Tina Sherwood

THE
ENCYCLOPEDIA
OF
POTTERY
TECHNIQUES

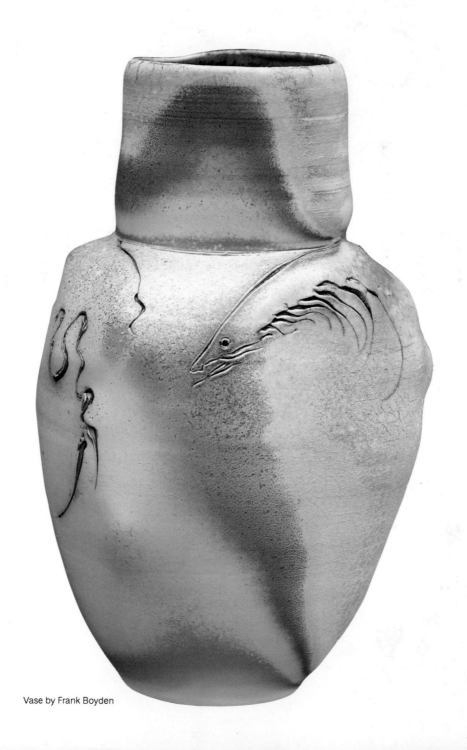

Vase by Frank Boyden

THE ENCYCLOPEDIA
OF
POTTERY TECHNIQUES

PETER COSENTINO

RUNNING PRESS
PHILADELPHIA · LONDON

A QUARTO BOOK

Copyright © 1990 Quarto Publishing plc

First published in the USA in 1990
by Running Press Book Publishers
125 South Twenty-second Street
Philadelphia, Pennsylvania 19103

ISBN 0-89471-892-4
9 8 7 6 5
Digit on the right indicates number of this printing

This book was designed and produced by
Quarto Publishing plc
The Old Brewery
6 Blundell Street
London N7 9BH

Senior Editor Kate Kirby
Editors Hazel Harrison, Laura Buller

Designer Bill Mason
Photography Ian Howes

Picture Researcher Rose Taylor

Art Director Moira Clinch
Assistant Art Director Chloë Alexander

Typeset by Ampersand Typesetters, Bournemouth
Manufactured in Hong Kong by Regent Publishing Services Ltd
Printed by Leefung-Asco Printers Ltd, China

My special thanks to Ian Howes whose skilful photography and inspired sense of
humour added much to the enjoyment of producing this book and to the many
potters who were kind enough to supply such a visual feast of quality work to
Quarto Publishing from which these examples were chosen.

This book may be ordered directly from the publisher. Please add $2.50 for postage
and handling for each copy, *but try your bookstore first.* Running Press Book
Publishers, 125 South Twenty-second Street, Philadelphia, Pennsylvania 19103.

This book is dedicated to Mandy, Thomas and Matthew

CONTENTS

FOREWORD

"No One So Much As You

Loves This My Clay,

Or Would Lament As You

Its Dying Day."

(From a love poem by Edward Thomas)

It is a lucky person who is able to spend his or her life in pursuit of that which is personally meaningful and relevant, and those few potters who can make a living by their craft are fortunate indeed. However, the idea of living by art or craft alone is largely a romantic myth, at any rate in modern times; and statistics issued by national craft associations highlight the pitifully low average annual wage of a full-time craftworker.

Until recently many potters were able to supplement the sales of their pots by teaching part-time. This to some extent removed the necessity of having to concentrate on commercially viable items, providing both an income and enough time to explore work of a more individual and personal nature. Many of these potters-teachers were to become important innovators and leaders in the field of studio ceramics.

In present-day financial climates, with reduced budgets and an apparently different idea of what some aspects of creative education are "worth," much of this stability has been lost – it is not uncommon, for example, to find full-time art and design courses offering their students no more than a single day's ceramic experience or even none.

There are fewer and fewer specialist pottery posts in schools, where pottery is often taught – if at all – by an art teacher. In elementary and high schools budgetary restraints often mean that buying a kiln is out of the question, while in the area of adult education there have been similar cutbacks. Many once-subsidized pottery classes can now only operate if they are self-supporting.

Set against this rather depressing scenario, however, is the fact that there is a growing interest in pottery, and many excellent books have appeared on the subject. Some are extremely informative, containing valuable information on processes, techniques, and behavior of materials, but in many cases they assume considerable prior knowledge of a craft which can appear technically complex and accordingly difficult to master. Rather than stimulating the reader, books of this nature sometimes frustrate the inexperienced by implying that only an elite group already initiated in the craft can expect to achieve anything worthwhile.

My own personal involvement with clay, as both potter and teacher, has given me an insight into what everyone can gain from an acquaintanceship with this fascinating material and the

processes associated with it, and this book has been written to enable the broadest possible readership to share this insight. It provides a glimpse into the fascinating world of pottery with its wealth of different techniques and individual approaches, and I hope it will encourage readers to discover for themselves the joys that lie in store for anyone who chooses to work with clay.

It is not aimed at potters of vast experience, since many are eminently more knowledgeable and qualified in many aspects of the craft than I am. It is for anyone who has ever considered trying their hand; anyone who has tried but been discouraged by seemingly difficult and complex processes; or anyone who has made a start and hungers for more. Only by continuing to introduce new generations to the creative potential of pottery can we guarantee the degree of interest needed for its continued survival, both as a recreational activity and as an important means of expressing our creative spirit.

While there is much to be gained by reading and finding out as much as possible about a particular activity, there can be no substitute for trying it yourself – Happy potting!

PETER COSENTINO

PART ONE

TECHNIQUES

The best pieces of pottery bring out in most of us an almost overwhelming desire to touch, caress, and hold them. For reasons often difficult to pinpoint, such works, whether ancient or contemporary, functional or abstract, appear to be "just right," seeming to possess a spirit of their own that draws us to them. When a piece of pottery appeals to us in this direct way, technicalities such as the type of clay used, the style of decoration, or the firing temperature seem of secondary importance; it is only when we try to analyze why we like or dislike an object that we begin to look more deeply at the techniques and processes involved in the journey from raw clay to the kiln. But the "spirit" of good pottery is no mere accident, it is the result of a harmonious bonding of the elements of design and technique through the knowledge and creativity of the potter.

The technical side of pottery can appear somewhat daunting, even disconcerting, and it is understandable that many students with only limited experience may initially seek to disguise their lack of technical competence by making things which primarily express their "creative" energies. But although knowledge of technique alone will produce nothing of lasting value, even the most abstract piece of pottery requires technical understanding. A piece may look so simple that one feels anyone with or without pottery experience could have made it, but in fact the potter was only able to achieve what he or she wanted through having a good grasp of certain important techniques.

Ideas are often sparked off by an investigation into technique and process, since these provide a basic framework for personal creativity. The aim in this first part of the book is to provide such a framework, and it sets out in alphabetical order the techniques most widely used by potters all over the world. A comprehensive range of techniques is represented in this section. Using step-by-step demonstrations and finished examples the book shows how to tackle the forming methods of throwing, slabbing, and pinching, and explains ways of decoration. The cross-referencing system will point you in the right direction if you need to know a little about one technique before you can tackle another.

I hope you will find this section useful and feel you want to try and experiment with some or all of the techniques yourself. However, although here each technique has been illustrated separately in the interests of clarity, this isolation of technique is far from desirable in practice. In reality, one technique merges with another, and most pieces of work will encompass several techniques in both construction and decoration, a fact clearly apparent in the wide range of potters' work shown throughout this book.

ADDITIVES

Clay in its naturally found state is rarely ideal for use by the potter, so other materials are added to make it behave in the way required. It may, for example, be either too plastic or not plastic enough; its color when fired might be too light, too dark, or simply unpleasant; it may not be able to withstand the temperature demanded of it during firing. All of these problems and numerous others can be solved by the addition of other ceramic materials, often no more complicated than the mixing of two or more different types of clay. Clay manufacturers and many individual potters mix clay bodies to their own particular recipes.

The addition of grog to clays (usually fired and ground fireclay obtainable in different grain sizes) and a whole variety of different colored sands are commonly used to minimize shrinkage, give extra strength to the clay, and improve both its texture and its color. Additives that alter the clay's physical properties in this way are normally introduced during the preparation or manufacturing stage. Coloring stains can be used to give precise colors to a clay. Some potters introduce materials that react in a dramatic way. The addition of materials which will fuse, bleed, or ooze out of the main clay body or glaze at temperatures below that required for the main body to mature can produce exciting effects, such as those seen in the work of potter Ewen Henderson.

A variety of different clays can be obtained from pottery suppliers, a small selection of which is shown here. These are specially prepared, and can be reliably expected to behave in predictable ways during forming and consequent firings. Although the fired color of most clays will be different from the pre-fired one, these will give an indication of the choices of color and texture open to the potter.

Top, left to right Porcelain, stoneware, red earthenware. Bottom, left to right: raku, crank mix, smooth stoneware.

Sands and grogs of varying coarseness can be used to add texture to clays or increase their strength and to some extent their color. Some grogs, such as the crushed red brick shown here, will only tolerate temperatures of up to 2012°F (1100°C), after which they will melt and bleed through to the clay surface.

Top, left to right Sand, coarse grog. Bottom, left to right: fine grog, red grog made from crushed brick.

To form interesting surface textures, combustible materials which will burn away during firing can be introduced into the clay, or they can be pressed into the surface while the clay is still pliable.

Where precise clay colors are required, coloring stains, or "body stains," can be mixed into clays. These are bought in powdered form, and are available in both bold and subtle hues. Unless a dark-colored clay is required, stains should be added to a white or light-colored base clay.

AGATEWARE

This is the name, derived from the agate stone which displays multicolored layers when sliced, given to pieces of work using a combination of contrasting colored clays for both decoration and as the integral structure. Certain techniques derived from carpentry, such as lamination and marquetry in clay (rather than wood), are also generally referred to as agateware. This technique offers the potter considerable scope since it permits both the creation of free, quick, and random effects, as when used in throwing, or enables extremely precise and carefully thought-out patterns and designs to be developed by hand-building construction methods.

Since clays of varying colors occur naturally, it would seem logical simply to select a variety of different clays and combine them to produce agateware effects. However, such a practice can produce disappointing results as many clays that look different in their plastic state will fire to very similar shades. Their shrinkage rates are also likely to differ, possibly causing them to crack or even separate during the initial drying or later firing stages. These problems, coupled with the desire for specific colors, usually lead potters to use one white or very light clay as their base clay to which they add colors in the form of stains or oxides. In order to disperse the color evenly throughout the clays and to prevent them from blistering when fired (unless, of course, such effects are particularly required) it is advisable to add the colorant to the clay while both are in powder form. The clay and colorant can then be mixed with water to form a slip which can then be sieved and prepared into a plastic state before use. The percentage of colorant required is a matter of personal taste, but as a very rough guide tests should be carried out using anything from 1-10% of colorant. The exception is the blues, which seldom require more than 2% for strong coloring. The increased popularity of the agateware technique in recent years has been recognized by pottery suppliers, who now offer prepared colored clays specifically for this purpose.

When agateware pieces are produced by joining strips or sections of colored clays, there is a danger of cracking along the many joints. The drying process is thus particularly critical, and should take place gradually, over a period of weeks rather than days. Work can be kept in plastic bags or containers in order to slow down drying once the piece is completed.

Agateware can either be glazed or left unglazed, possibly burnished. The potter will have decided on the look of the finished piece beforehand, and that decision will probably determine the choice and strength of the colors used. Pale colors, for example, could be totally obscured by anything other than a transparent glaze (some colorants such as copper only come to life when covered in glaze), yet be quite striking when left unglazed. Conversely, a harsh or strong color might be at its best when it is bleeding through a lightly colored or white matt glaze.

Agateware requires the use of two or more different colored clays. A more or less infinite range of bold or subtle colors can be obtained by using body stains.

2 Slicing through the block of clays will reveal the extent to which they have blended together. Strong agate patterning is usually the result of a smaller ratio of the stronger color.

Combining different colored clays

1 Two or more clays of different colors can be combined for throwing by the techniques of kneading and wedging. Clays to be used in this way should be well prepared separately beforehand, as prolonged wedging and kneading of different colors will blend them all together.

3 You will not be able to see the agate effect during throwing, as the surface will develop an overall color.

4 The agate patterning will become clearly visible when the pot is turned at the leather-hard stage. The random nature of this effect during throwing ensures that every piece is different.

Using strips of clay
1 Ideas for pattern combinations can be worked out initially by using modeling clay, as colored clays are both expensive and time-consuming to prepare. Working with modeling clay also makes you realize how easily colors can be contaminated.

2 Strips from clays of different colors can be joined together to form slabs of patterned clay. All the strips should be in a similar state of plasticity, and guides will ensure an even thickness during rolling. The blade used to cut the strips must be sharp or the clay may tear.

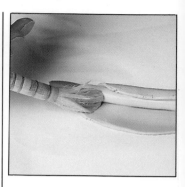

4 Alternating layers of colored clay are wrapped around each other, and a little water is used to help the layers to bond. Each layer should be rolled firmly to expel any air bubbles trapped between them.

The author combined porcelain with red earthenware clay to produce this burnished and unglazed piece. In order to prevent the separation of the two clays during drying, the pot was allowed to dry very gradually over a period of weeks rather than days.

3 Colored slip made from the clay being used is applied thickly to the scored surface before a further strip is added. The colored slip used as "glue" will be visible as a thin, delicate line once the final scraping has been done. The growing slab of agate clay is gently but firmly squeezed between two wooden slats to ensure secure joints between each strip.

5 Once sliced, these multi-colored coil sections can either be left rounded or pressed into triangular, rectangular, or other geometric shapes before use. It is wise to prepare all the sections you will need before beginning to make anything, so that your work flow is not interrupted by having to stop and make more.

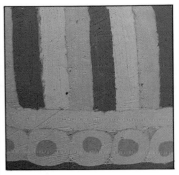

6 Agate pieces can be formed inside a mold or other suitable former. The shape is carefully built up by scoring each individual section and pressing it into place. At this stage the pattern may not appear to be crisp, but this will be remedied at the scraping stage.

7 The work should be dried extremely slowly to give all the separate pieces time to join properly. It should not be removed from the former until stiff enough to handle without fear of damage or distortion.

8 When at least leather-hard it can be removed, though the inside can be cleaned up by scraping beforehand. A flexible metal tool can be useful, but sandpaper or steel wool are more suitable if the work has dried beyond leather-hard. A face mask should be worn in order to avoid the risk of inhaling powdered clay.

9 The blue-colored slurry or slip used to join each section together is visible as a fine line between each joined section.

These two deep bowls by Judith Wooton illustrate the precise control of patterning it is possible to achieve by this combination of forming and decorative technique.

ALTERING THROWN SHAPES

Because of the nature of the forming process, wheel-thrown pots are round and symmetrical. However, the potter can alter this original shape once the process of throwing is complete. This should never be seen as a means of disguising a poorly thrown shape (it is in any case rarely possible to disguise off-centered work, as this fault will still be seen). Altering a thrown shape should be a positive intention, not an afterthought.

One of the simplest methods of alteration is to exert gentle, even pressure with the palms, squashing the wet form gradually from opposite sides and so creating an oval. If a form is thin it may have to be left to stiffen slightly before any alteration is made, or the dynamic tension of the shape may be lost. If more severe shape alteration is required, it may be necessary to throw the form without a base (which can be added later), or remove sections of the base to prevent it from tearing under pressure. In some cases, this may only involve slicing through the point where the wall joins the base.

The altering of thrown shapes also has many practical applications in the production of functional domestic ware. It is common practice, for example, for potters to make oval thrown casserole dishes by completely removing an elliptical section from the base before forcing the hole to seal as the rounded shape is formed into an oval one. A thrown form can also be altered in shape by introducing one or more additional sections. These can either be thrown or produced by other techniques.

1 Gently squashing a freshly thrown form will produce an oval shape. The rims of bottles and even bowls can be altered in this way.

These two bottle forms by Lucie Rie have flattened necks which result in elliptical rims, creating a subtle contrast to the simple, rounded qualities of the body. The clay used for these pieces has been loaded with manganese, which can be seen as specks of color bleeding through the creamy glaze.

2 Where a whole section of a thrown form is to be flattened, it may be necessary to first release the wall from its base. Cut through it with a needle at the point where it is level with the inside base height.

3 The wall, freed from its base, can now be pushed inward, producing a flattened side.

4 Once flattening is complete, the wall and base can be rejoined. If this is done soon after throwing while the clay is still soft, there is no need to apply slurry; the wall and base can be joined by merging the two together with a wooden rib.

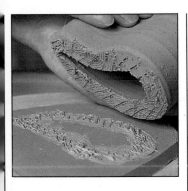

5 Where dramatic shape alteration is required, it is often necessary to throw a baseless "sleeve," which can be altered and then attached to a base once the shaping has been done. This prevents the base from buckling or splitting open during shaping.

This striking black form made by Hans Coper incorporates flattened thrown sections as part of its construction. The various thrown elements or composite parts have been skilfully combined to produce a unified whole.

7 Oval-shaped casserole dishes are popular with many domestic potters. A rounded dish can be turned into an oval by removing an elliptical section. The edges of the hole are then scored, slurry is added, and the hole is closed up by pressure on the outside of the walls. To help the sides to close easily, this needs to be done on a wet, non-absorbent surface, as otherwise there may be distortion.

8 Once the hole in the base is closed, a smoothing tool can be used to ensure a good seal and a smooth base. Any additional smoothing to the underside of the base can be carried out when the dish is leather-hard.

6 A natural development of this technique is to throw two or more similar baseless sleeves which can then be cut, opened out and joined together after shaping. Secure the joins with slurry applied over scoring to assist bonding. As soon as the shape is stiff enough, it can be joined onto a rolled slab of clay for the base.

Slabbed sections can be introduced to thrown pieces, with the rigid nature of the added section creating a contrast to the more fluid thrown one. This piece is by the author.

APPLIED DECORATION

Clay can be added or "applied" to the surface of a piece of work as a decorative effect at any stage until the work becomes leather-hard, at which point any clay additions are likely to crack or fall away from the surface during the drying and firing processes. Applied decoration may take the form of loose, random patterns or repeating ones such as SPRIGG DECORATION. Many contemporary potters make sparing use of simple pellets or small coil additions to enhance such features as spouts, handles, and lids, or to create subtle breaks in otherwise plain surfaces. The use of applied surface decoration as a means of creating large areas of textured patterning and low-relief modeling can be seen throughout the whole history of pottery up to the present. Many examples are to be found in medieval English pottery as well as that of many less developed societies today.

Whether a single pellet is to be applied or a whole surface of low relief created, the clay surface is first scored and slurry is applied before pressing the decoration firmly in place.

The application of additional clay sometimes forms part of the production of abstract or non-functional pieces of work. In such cases the "additions" play a vital role in the actual form and structure of the piece of work rather than being a purely decorative feature. The work of Colin Pearson illustrates this quite clearly: the added "wings" are more than simply a decorative feature, they are an integral part of the piece.

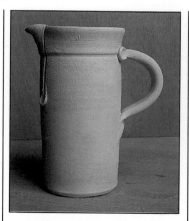

1 A single pellet of clay can be used to good effect either to break up large, plain areas of a clay surface, or simply to act as a "stop" on incised lines. Pellets or other pieces of clay are also often used decoratively, applied at points where handles or spouts are attached to the main body of the pot.

2 A single pellet can be attached to form a finger or thumb grip on the handles of vessels such as mugs and jugs. Potters appear to be divided in their preference for downward or upward-pointing grips.

Applied decoration to create texture

Whole areas of textured pattern can be built by using a variety of small clay shapes, which can range from pellets to thin coils. Where soft clay is applied to a soft surface, it is not always necessary to apply slurry first, but once the surface becomes leather-hard, both slurry and scoring will be needed before the decoration is applied.

▼The applied decoration—in this instance made from a sprigg mold—is an appropriate surface treatment of this thrown bread crock by potter Kenneth Bright.

BANDING

As its name implies, banding means applying lines or bands of color around a symmetrical form. It can be done at any stage of the process, from before the construction of the piece is complete right through the many stages that follow – even after successive firings.

A heavy turntable called a banding wheel, specially designed for this technique, is a useful aid, although banding can be successfully done on a potter's wheel. A variety of brushes are also made for banding, which hold enough colored slip or pigment to allow a whole band to be laid on without the need to refill midway. The type of colorant used will be determined by the stage in the ceramic process that a particular piece of work has reached. Colored slips can be used from the wet state to the dry (some specially formulated slips can even be used on a bone-dry surface), and once the piece of work is bone dry or bisque fired, metallic oxides or underglaze colors can be painted on. Oxides and onglaze colors can be used on glazed pieces immediately prior to the glaze firing. Once the glaze firing is complete, onglaze enamel colors and lusters can be banded onto the surface and then refired.

Banding on its own rarely forms exciting decorative effects, and is perhaps best known for the part it plays in such techniques as MAJOLICA, where bands of color are often used to separate highly decorative areas of brushwork.

1 Banding can be carried out on freshly thrown pots still on the wheel, or pots can be left to stiffen and be turned before banding. In either case colored slips can be used.

2 Once a pot has been bisque fired, underglaze colors can be banded onto the surface. Where thin lines are required, it is important to ensure that the brush takes up enough colorant for a complete rotation, thus giving a flowing, uninterrupted line. A heavy banding wheel rather than a lightweight turntable should be used whenever possible, as the rotation is much steadier.

3 Banding can also be done immediately after glazing and before glaze firing. The soft and absorbent surface is very vulnerable at this stage, however, so great care must be taken not to chip or damage the glaze covering.

This delicately thrown lustered porcelain bowl by Mary Rich employs banding as an effective means of separating and defining highly patterned layers of gold geometric designs. Her work reflects the influences of the decorative wares of Islam and other Eastern cultures.

BEATING (PADDLING)

While clay is in a soft, pliable state it will respond to pressure exerted on it. Repeatedly hitting pliable clay, regardless of the tool used (it could simply be your own hands), will automatically alter its shape. Throwers sometimes beat the sides of pots to produce flattened surfaces (see FACETING), while hand-builders often beat or "paddle" the shape they are working on as a method of construction. It causes the clay wall to thin and grow as it is beaten, and also firmly welds together any joints. Perhaps its greatest potential, however, lies in the fact that beating clay with any type of tool will inevitably leave some sort of marks on the surface. This can be used to produce a range of rich surface textures whose only limits are imposed by individual imagination and resourceful-ness – anything and everything can become a beating tool. Although beating can be regarded as a form of impressed decoration (see IMPRESSING), it is a technique that is likely to produce far more fluid and spontaneous surface patterns.

1 Beating, or paddling, can be a useful technique to use during coiling. Thick sections can be treated in this way, thinning and increasing the height of the pot as well as helping the coils to merge together.

2 The shape of a thrown form can be modified or altered quite dramatically by beating while the clay is still pliable enough to respond without cracking. Virtually anything can be used for beating, although the implement should have a porous surface to prevent it from sticking to the clay.

3 The soft, yielding surface of clay is ideal for creating textures. Here they are made by beating with a rough-edged piece of wood.

4 Paddles made from pieces of wood wrapped with rope or string can produce bold or subtle markings in the soft clay.

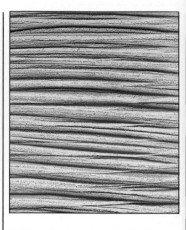

5 There is almost no limit to the different surface textures and patterns obtainable by the simple technique of beating, and such surfaces can be used to form the basis of exciting work (also see SLABBING).

6 Here a very fine-textured pattern has been created by beating.

BURNISHING

The technique of burnishing the surface of pottery as a means of partially sealing it when fired at low temperatures can be traced back to ancient civilizations, and is still used in many undeveloped societies. Arising from practical necessity, it has gained recent popularity throughout the USA and Europe as a decorative technique. Burnishing involves no more than rubbing the clay surface with a smooth tool to produce a mirror-smooth surface. It is done when the clay surface is leather-hard or dry, and has a compressing effect on the clay particles. Most clays are suitable for burnishing, although the finer the clay, the smoother the burnished surface; coarse-bodied ones will throw up pieces of grog or sand which will continually scratch the surface. The surface color will be determined by the color of the clay itself, so unless colored slips are to be applied over the surface prior to burnishing, a clay with a pleasing color should be chosen.

Suitable tools for burnishing include smooth rounded pebbles, the convex side of metal spoons, smooth metal knife handles, wooden modeling tools, and even inflated sections from bubble packaging. The type of tools chosen will largely depend on the shape of the pots to be burnished; potters who make use of this technique quickly develop their own personal favorites for particular jobs. Although it is perhaps easiest to burnish when the pot reaches leather-hard state, the shiny surface will often sink as the pot dries out completely. A dry pot with a fine spray of water over the surface will produce a more durable gloss, while even better results are produced by coating the surface of the dry pot with a thin slip which will adhere to the surface without flaking off as it dries. Burnishing dry pots is likely to produce more breakages as during this dry state the pot is at its most brittle and vulnerable.

There is no right or wrong way to burnish clay surfaces: some potters work in small circular movements, and others work vertically, horizontally, or a combination of all three. The important thing is to ensure the whole surface of the pot is worked on unless parts are to be left purposely unburnished.

Once dry, the burnished pot can be fired in a normal bisque firing (see FIRING), which should not exceed 1742°F (950°C) or the shine will diminish. Alternately burnished pots can be fired in a sawdust firing which will give them a variegated blackened finish (see SMOKING). Once the pot has been fired it can either be left without further treatment or polished with oils or a thin coating of wax to enhance the shine.

1 A variety of objects can form useful burnishing tools, and potters soon develop their own favorites. These could include such unlikely items as pieces of bubble packing material and dentist's tools as well as the more obvious spoons, pebbles, and knife handles.

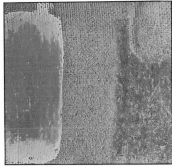

3 Here the convex surface of a spoon is used in small circular movements for the outside surface. The same method can be employed for the insides of bowl shapes.

2 A knife handle used vertically on a surface of uncomplicated shape can burnish large areas effectively and quickly.

4 Coarse clays will throw up pieces of grog which will scratch the surface, but fine slips can be applied over them to allow successful burnishing.

5 Dry pots can either be lightly sprayed with water and then burnished immediately afterwards, or the dry surface can be covered with a suitable colored slip before burnishing.

7 After bisque firing, burnished pots can be lightly waxed. This helps to seal the surfaces as well as deepening the gloss.

6 Burnishing dry rather than leather-hard surfaces produces a high gloss which is less likely to dull afterward.

The work of Magdalene Odundo forges a link between the simple traditional hand-forming and burnishing techniques often employed on African utilitarian wares and the more sophisticated approach of Western potters, some of whose work exploits pure form rather than function.

CENTERING

This is the process used to ensure that the clay revolves in the exact center of the wheelhead prior to THROWING. It is arguably the most important factor in successful throwing, for unless this first step is mastered, the result is likely to be walls of uneven thickness, weak areas, and poor, unstable shapes. Centering can be achieved through a number of different styles and varying hand positions, and with experience an individual's personal preference will emerge.

The state of the clay you use for throwing is very important. It should always be well prepared and of an even consistency (see KNEADING and WEDGING). Although it is easier to practice centering with soft clay, if it is too soft, it will be difficult to throw with once the centering is done. If the clay is too stiff it will be unresponsive, will require far more effort on the potter's part, and may cause twisting of walls in later throwing.

1 The clay should be well prepared, slapped into a ball shape, and then placed firmly as near to the center of the wheelhead as possible (the closer it is, the easier the process will be). Slowly rotate the wheelhead and pat the clay into an even-shaped dome.

2 Rotating the wheel quickly, lubricate both hands and clay, and apply pressure from the outer edge of both palms positioned at opposite sides. Both hands must simultaneously force the clay mass up into a cone.

3 Coning assists the process of getting the whole clay mass into the center as well as helping to ensure an even consistency by bringing any air pockets to the surface. The cone should be depressed by cupping the apex with the working hand with the other hand supporting it and exerting slight inward pressure on the cone as it is pushed downwards. Coning should be done several times before the final centering movement.

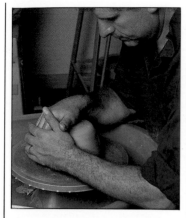

4 Hand positions for the final centering rely on stability, so the arms should be resting on the wheel tray. Exert downward pressure on the clay with the working hand while pulling the clay mass directly towards you with the other. Pressure must be simultaneous, the wheel should be rotating quickly, and hands should be linked to support the body effort.

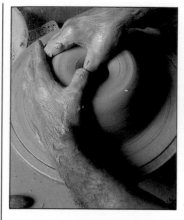

6 Experienced potters will know intuitively when the clay feels centered. A simple check can be made, however, by approaching the rotating mass gradually with a tool or finger and checking that during the complete revolution it rotates an equal distance from the clay. The clay should not be opened up until it is well centered; if it is not, the final process should be repeated.

5 An alternative method for final centering is to exert pressure in a sideways direction horizontally across the wheelhead with the working hand while bearing down on the clay mass with the other. Again, both movements must be simultaneous.

Even when dramatic alteration to a thrown shape is envisaged, as in this form by the author, it is important that the initial shape is the product of a well-centered piece of clay – as any alteration is more likely to accentuate rather than hide any previous throwing fault. This piece, which was altered directly after throwing, has been coated with layers of colored slips spattered onto the surface with an old toothbrush and burnished when dry.

7 This section, taken from a dish thrown with poorly centered clay, shows quite clearly the resultant uneven thicknesses in the wall.

COILING

This is the technique of building forms from coils – "snakes" or ropes of clay. The clay must be well prepared (see KNEADING and WEDGING) before use and should be soft and pliable enough to roll and shape without cracking. It should also have a reasonable sand and grog content to lessen the risk of warping and cracking during drying and consequent firings.

Coils can be rolled by hand or extruded (see EXTRUSION). It is advisable to prepare a good quantity before building begins (these can be kept wrapped in polyethylene to prevent them from drying out) so that concentration and flow are not interrupted by the need to make more coils. A turntable or whirler is useful for coiling, and a suitable board covered with paper or fabric to work on will minimize the risk of damage to the work when it has to be moved.

For handmade coils, begin by forming rough clay ropes, and roll them on an absorbent surface to prevent sticking.

A clay base can be formed by patting out a piece of the clay used for the coils, after which successive coils are welded into each other from the inside by merging almost half the width of the upper coil into the one underneath. The outside can be left in partial or complete coil form, although the joining will be most successful if the outer surface is also welded. If the shape is to grow straight up, coils are placed directly on top of one another. For a swelling shape each coil is placed slightly on the outer edge of the one before it, while the reverse procedure will narrow the shape.

The shape can be supported by loosely packing the inside with crumpled newspaper as it grows, but be careful not to encourage too dramatic an alteration of shape or the form may collapse. TEMPLATES can be made from stiff cardboard or thin board and used to ensure a predetermined profile, and molds or formers can also be used, although such aids tend to produce a rather mechanical quality not in keeping with the gentle, contemplative quality of the technique.

It is not always possible, or even desirable, to complete a coil pot in a single session, particularly if it is a large or complex shape. In this case, the lower sections can be left to dry out slightly while the working section is kept moist with a damp cloth and polyethylene. The first coil to be added in a new working session should be applied with scoring and slurry to assist joining, after which further coils can be joined directly onto each other.

1 The first step towards rolling coils is to squeeze out rough clay ropes.

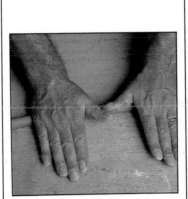

2 Roll out the coils with the palms of your hands, working on a porous surface to which the clay will not stick. Make sure that the coil completes a revolution before being rolled back, as this will keep it round in section rather than flattened or oval. Keep the coils to an even thickness, and make enough of them to complete the piece of work.

3 Join the coil firmly to the clay base by welding it in with your finger. Work on a board and turntable if possible, and use the supporting hand to prevent the shape from spreading outward.

4 It is important to join and smooth in each coil on the inside of the pot as it is positioned. If a smooth outer surface is required, coils should be welded on the outside also.

5 Coils should not be joined at the same point on each successive layer, or weaknesses will develop. A tight joint can be made by cutting through the coil ends at an angle so that they slot together.

7 Conversely, if the shape is required to narrow, successive coils should be positioned slightly on the inside edge of the previous one.

▲ The coiled vessels of Fiona Salazar incorporate brightly colored symbols and motifs painted in colored slips. She begins by throwing the bases and then adds the coils.

▼ David Roberts's bottle forms, with their gently rounded, swollen shapes, reflect the calm, contemplative qualities associated with coiling. He works on a small group of pots at the same time, so they all have a direct relationship. The blackened lines on the surface glaze are the result of raku firing.

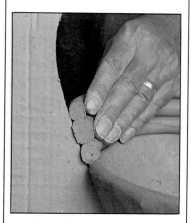

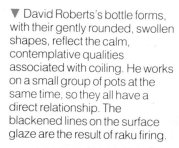

6 If necessary a template can be made to ensure that a pre-determined shape develops, though this can give a rather mechanical and sterile effect. If the shape is to grow outward, each successive coil should be placed slightly on the outer edge of the previous one, as shown here.

8 The coils can form both the structure and the decoration of the pot. Here a soft coil has been formed into a wavy patterned section. This should be sealed and smoothed on the inside only. A plain coil is used here to separate the patterned bands, helping to ensure that the layers are properly sealed and level. When patterned coils are used, even greater care must be taken to seal the inside, or cracks and fractures may appear after drying or firing.

COLLARING

Wheel-thrown shapes can be narrowed or totally enclosed to produce bottle forms or hollow spheres by compressing the clay shape. Collaring is sometimes even more graphically referred to as "throttling" the clay, a reference to the hand positions used for this technique which narrow the shape while simultaneously thickening the clay wall.

Collaring works against the natural inclinations of the wheel, which naturally spreads the clay outwards, and to be successful the clay must be in good working condition. If not it may buckle or become uneven around the rim area, a common problem. Clay which has been worked for too long a period or is very thin may refuse to be collared. The section to be worked on should be coaxed in gradual stages rather than be forced to narrow, and the wheel should rotate quickly.

Because collaring produces a compression of the clay, it can be utilized to add height through further throwing, a technique also employed in the throwing of spouts.

Narrowing of shapes during throwing can also take place by lifting in a slightly inward rather than vertical direction.

1 Exerting inward restricting pressure on a thrown form is referred to as collaring. The hand positions used have given rise to the apt alternative term, "throttling."

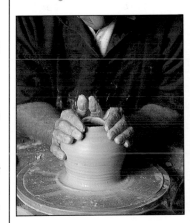

2 Continued collaring can produce forms with narrow openings or even totally enclosed ones. For successful collaring, the clay must be in good condition, and the wheelhead needs to rotate quickly. Clay that is worked for long periods may tire, which can cause it to buckle.

3 Collaring thickens the area as well as narrowing it, and the extra thickness can be used to increase height.

The collaring technique is used for thrown narrow-necked shapes. This large swollen-bellied cider jar by John Leach was collared to reduce its width and produce a well-defined neck and top. Both pieces are wood-fired stoneware, the variation of color being the result of direct contact with the flames.

COLORING

Styles and tastes in pottery are ever changing, and while there still is – and should always be – a place for the quiet pot whose muted earthy colors blend discreetly into its surroundings, more bright colors are now seen.

Color in pottery is achieved by the use of various metal oxides. Clay stains or colorants derived from metal oxides can be mixed into the clay to alter its basic color before use, common examples of this technique being Wedgwood's blue and green jasperware and black basaltware. Liquid clays with additions of oxides to form colored slips or "engobes" can either color the whole surface by completely covering it or can be applied as a decorative effect (see SLIP DECORATION and GLAZING) prior to bisque firing. In either case, glaze can be applied on top. Specially prepared underglaze colors or metal oxides can be painted or sprayed onto dry or bisque pottery prior to glazing, when the colors achieve their full richness. Metal oxides or in-glaze color derivatives can be introduced to a glaze to produce a particular color once the glaze firing is complete, or alternately a piece of pottery can be painted or sprayed with oxides after glazing but before firing (see DRAWING and MAJOLICA). Once pottery has been glaze fired, onglaze colors or enamels can be applied to the surface and refired at a low temperature to set them (see FIRING).

Iron, copper, cobalt, manganese, chromium, nickel, vanadium, ilmenite, and rutile are the most commonly used metal oxides from which most ceramic colors are derived.

▲ Sandy Brown's plate displays an artistic and expressionistic use of bold, often raw, color. She uses a variety of metallic oxides and commercial stains to decorate the surface of her work to produce lively, uninhibited surfaces.

◀ Colorants such as oxides and an almost infinite number of specially prepared glaze stains can be added to glazes to produce all-over color. The strong yellow on this porcelain bowl by Lucie Rie was achieved by adding uranium oxide to the glaze.

◄ Subtle, earthy coloring is an important element of the work of Michael Bayley, which reflects his love of the natural landscape. He achieves his range of colors – from creams to dark browns – by adding iron, manganese oxide, and a variety of sands and grogs to his clay.

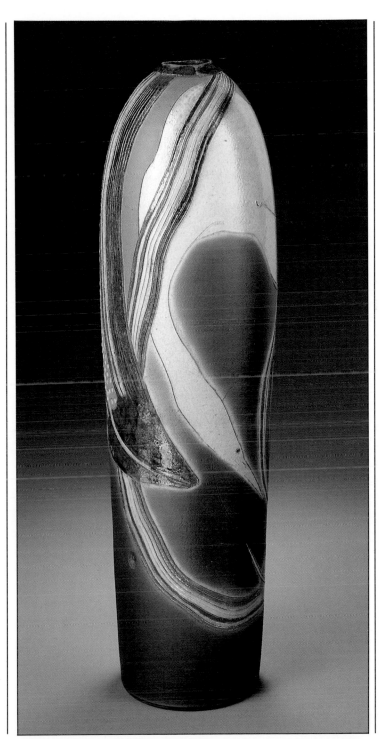

▲ The combination of decorative methods, application of slips, oxides, and colorants, under- and overglaze painting, and the overlaying and overlapping of many different colored glazes all contribute to the rich palette of color which is a feature of the work of potter John Glick.

► This raku fired Heron and Carp Vase is by Frank Boyden, a potter who skilfully employs a combination of slips, glaze, and firing technique to achieve the colorful and decorative visual contrasts in his work. The blackened areas are a result of the unglazed areas being "reduced" during the raku process.

COMBING

This technique involves cutting parallel lines into the clay surface, and can be done with any toothed implement. An ordinary kitchen fork, a plastic comb, or broken sections from saw blades are all ideal, while for specific effects you can, of course, cut out your own combing tools from stiff cardboard or odd pieces of hardboard. Combing can be carried out at any point from wet right through to very dry, but before the bisque firing (see FIRING).

The technique is effective both on its own and when used in conjunction with SLIP DECORATION. The combing reveals the original body color beneath the slip, a quick and simple decorative technique often employed by throwers who are producing large numbers of simple shapes on a repetitive basis.

Burrs of clay will form along the combed lines, which are best removed with a stiff, dry brush to reveal crisp lines. This should be done when the surface has dried to at least leather-hard, or there is a danger of damaging the clarity of the lines.

1 A variety of odds and ends such as old forks or pieces from saw blades make useful combing tools. This decorative technique can be carried out directly onto the clay surface or through a colored slip, which reveals the original clay underneath.

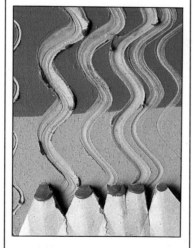

2 Stiff pieces of cardboard can be cut to produce "teeth" of varying sizes, which produce interesting variations when used for combing.

In this piece by the author a section of saw blade was used to comb across the pot's surface in both vertical and horizontal directions when the clay was leather-hard. The textural effect was emphasized by rubbing in manganese, and white slip was then brushed over the raised surface.

DECORATING

The world of pottery and ceramics changes so rapidly that it is difficult, if not impossible, to keep up with fresh developments in style and decorative technique. Good potters show a healthy awareness of the techniques that have become standard worldwide, while also frequently delving into past practices and bringing fresh insight to the use of many obscure techniques and the styles and decorative methods of other cultures.

In recent years there has been a welcome increase in the availability of pottery literature, illustrating the ways in which potters continue to push and test existing boundaries of technique, ingenuity, and imagination. A further influence has been the dramatic shift towards a broader acceptance of the role played by the designer within the field of art and design education. Many potters have fine art rather than craft backgrounds, having found in pottery and ceramics a suitable vehicle for personal expression. Ideas and imagination may once have been stifled by the inability to achieve a particular result, but this is certainly not the case today – suppliers can provide excellent materials and an ever-increasing palette of color, which has been partly responsible for the impressively artistic approach seen in much of the pottery decoration today.

▲ The highly colorful decorative surfaces of this functional group owe much to the skills of Janice Tchalenko, who played a prominent part in establishing the Dart Pottery as a commercial pottery with strong roots in studio traditions. This bright decoration was achieved through a combination of brushing, trailing, and sponging techniques.

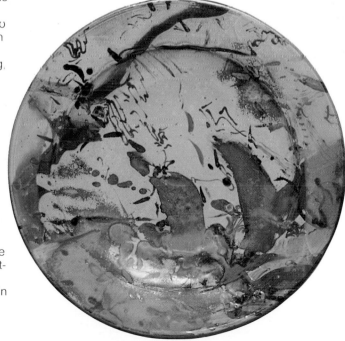

▶ The inventive decorative techniques of John Glick involve overlaying a number of different-colored glazes to which further color is added in the form of stain and oxides. This results in rich surfaces filled with color and vitality.

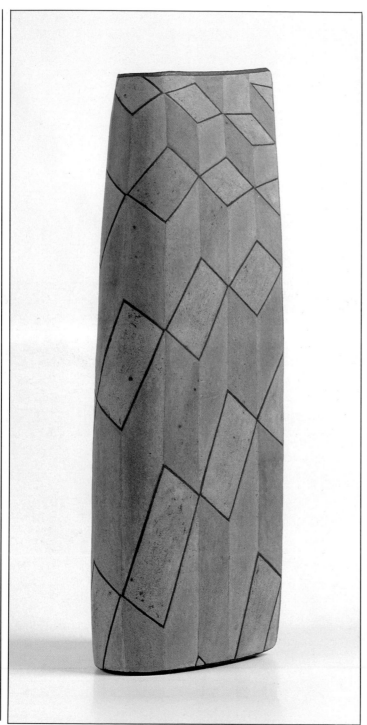

▶ John Gibson's decorative techniques – combing, stamping, resist, and various methods of applying color by slip trailing and underglaze applications – are all carried out while his work is in the greenware stage, that is at the stage before being bisque fired. They combine harmoniously to produce highly decorative yet functional surfaces.

◀ The precise slip-decorated surfaces of Elizabeth Fritsch's hand-built pots are carefully planned to produce visual ambiguity through the controlled use of optical illusions generated by the use of geometric designs.

▼ The work of Dennis Parks incorporates strong narrative elements which are reflected through his carefully decorated surfaces. This large thrown plate, about 20in. (51cm) in diameter, is entitled Anecdote of the Flask.

◄ Daphne Carnegy's decorative brushwork and application of color by means of on-glaze, or majolica, techniques have strong associations with the traditional tin-glazed wares found throughout Europe. Her forms and her fluid, artistic approach to surface decoration, however, give her work a contemporary flavor.

► The highly decorative inlay technique employed by Jo Connell is inseparable from the actual construction process. The large motifs and strongly contrasting colored clays serve to produce a bold, distinctive pattern.

DESIGNING

Design can refer to specific patterns and decoration or to the carefully planned development of a piece of pottery, but here I use the word in its broad sense, to describe the development of individual ideas taken from a particular starting point through to the completed work. Once some level of technical competence has been achieved, the real journey begins, that of progressing from how to make something towards what is to be made. However, design can never be separated from process: the potter must consider all the stages each piece has to go through.

Potters' inspiration comes from as many different sources as any other artist's, so it is impossible to list each one. However, natural forms, animals, the human figure, the local environment, or mechanical objects are all good starting points for the development of ideas and themes. In functional pottery, practical considerations obviously play an important part in the design process, but individual style is just as important as it is in abstract pieces that have no such constraints.

Whatever the source of ideas, the recording of information is part of the design process, and potters, like artists, keep sketchbooks which they use as reference when developing ideas for new pieces. Such books reveal a vast diversity of stimulus which can range from a closely observed section of a seed pod to nothing more than a personal response to a color which made some impact on the senses for a brief moment.

The simple immediacy of these swan sketches (right) taken from pages of Mary Wondrausch's sketchbook is skilfully translated into ceramic terms through the strong, linear quality clearly visible in her sgraffito decorated bowl (below). In this piece, the swans are cleverly incorporated onto the inner surface and occupy virtually all the space as they appear to jostle for position. Simple sketches are a very effective means of developing such design ideas, and are commonly employed by potters in much the same way as an artist undertakes a series of preparatory studies in order to develop a composition.

▼ Karen Chesney's bird vases demonstrate the interplay between function, form, and decoration. In this example function plays a secondary role to the highly decorative nature of the piece, which incorporates colored slips, resist techniques, and lusters.

◄ Design for domestic pottery must take into account both decoration and the fact that each piece has to fulfil a particular function. This attractive dinner service by Daphne Carnegy successfully combines functional qualities with a personal style of decoration.

▼ Once functional constraints are removed, design criteria can become more personal. Sandy Brown's stoneware piece, Horse and Dancer, although undoubtedly figurative, emphasizes expressive content.

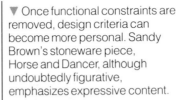

▲ In non-functional pieces there is often an open and direct visual relationship between the source of inspiration and the finished piece. This raku piece by Christa-Maria Herrmann, fittingly called Driftwood Ball, clearly shows its design origins.

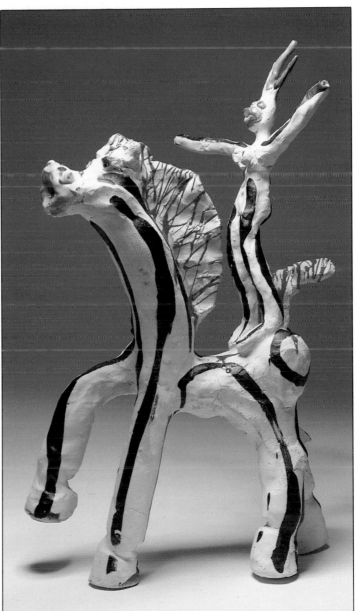

DRAWING

Virtually any drawing technique can be used on clay as long as ceramic pigment or specially made ceramic pencils or crayons are used. The numerous drying and firing stages offer a further variation in surface quality, because designs can be drawn at each stage, resulting in different final effects.

While the clay surface is still in a plastic state, lines can be drawn into the surface with any implement that will make a mark.

The surface of the clay alters once it has dried out fully or has been bisque fired. It is still possible to scratch into these surfaces, but better results will be obtained by drawing on them with coloring oxides or underglaze colors mixed with water (see COLORING) or ceramic pencils or crayons. At this stage, the clay surface is very absorbent and reacts in a similar way to blotting paper if colorants are mixed with excessive amounts of water.

Perhaps the most popular stage for drawing and painting onto clay surfaces is immediately after GLAZING but before glaze firing (see FIRING). The surface will react to pigment mixed with water in almost the same way as watercolor paper. Any marks made will sink into and blend slightly with the glaze surface during the glaze firing, producing a slightly softened line. A whole range of colors can be used, including alternative glazes which can be applied by brush or slip trailer (see GLAZING and SLIP DECORATION).

Using a sharp instrument
1 While the clay is soft or leather-hard, a sharp instrument can be used to draw into and etch the surface. Surfaces treated in this way can be left with the drawing clearly visible or used simply as a means of defining areas to be filled with color at a later stage.

2 Drawn pictures can be built up into low-relief designs by the addition of clay if the surface is still soft enough to permit it.

Using a brush
1 After bisque firing, pictures can be drawn onto the porous surface with a suitable brush.

2 Although applying a transparent glaze will initially seem to hide the picture, once glaze-fired it will reappear with no loss of detail and a gloss finish.

White glazed surfaces are ideal for decorating with a combination of drawing and painting techniques, as demonstrated by Andrew McGarva's Fish Dish.

DUSTING

This is the process of applying glaze to pottery in powder form. It was a technique commonly used for applying galena lead glazes to slip-decorated dishes in England during the seventeenth century. Galena glazes were harmful to health and safety, and are no longer used, but the method can still be employed as long as care is taken to ensure that no glaze dust is inhaled. It is thus necessary to wear a face mask.

Dusting is best carried out on a damp, unfired pot whose surface will absorb the dry glaze powder. For this reason it is sometimes used in conjunction with raw glazing (see GLAZING). A simple method is to put a small amount of powdered glaze into a sieve and, holding it over the pot surface, gently vibrate the sieve to encourage the glaze particles to fall onto the pot's surface. Alternatively, a brush can be used to push the glaze powder through the mesh.

Here a powdered glaze is applied to the surface of a suitable pot by manually vibrating a sieve. A face mask should be worn, as it is dangerous to inhale the glaze-dust particles.

During the seventeenth century, dusting was a popular means of applying galena glazes. Traditional slipware designs like this one by Thomas Toft were often glazed in this manner.

EXTRUSION

This is a clay-forming technique involving forcing clay through shaped dies or templates, traditionally used to produce building materials such as blocks, pipes, insulators, and even roofing tiles. Its potential has not been missed by the studio potter.

The simplest forms of extrusion are pushing soft clay through a coarse-meshed sieve or bending a piece of stiff wire into a small loop and passing it through a block of clay. Types of hand extruders such as pug mills (see KNEADING) and even meat grinders, are commonly used to produce solid shaped sections for handles or for COILING, the shape of the section determined by the shape of the die the clay is forced through.

Narrow sheets or strips of clay can be produced for SLABBING, and if coarse clay is used, the resulting section can be sliced off to form tiles. However, strips formed in this way are prone to warping during drying unless turned frequently. Curved sections which can be formed into spheres can also be extruded with offset semi-circular apertures.

With special dies consisting of an inner plate bridged to an outer plate with space between the two, hollow sections of virtually any shape can be extruded. The gap between the two die plates will determine the wall thickness of the extruded section. A hollow section can be altered in shape while sufficiently pliable, split and opened to form a sheet of clay, or simply left as a cylinder (see THROWING), with a base added from a further section.

1 The effect of clay extrusion at its most basic level can be demonstrated very simply by pushing a soft piece of clay through a coarse-meshed sieve. Each of the resulting strands viewed separately will reflect the shape and size of the mesh used.

2 A variety of die plates is available for extruding clay sections of different shapes and sizes. The "spider" attachment seen in the center of the photograph enables hollow sections to be formed.

3 Extruded solid sections can be used, among other things, for coiling or for handles for both thrown and hand-built pots.

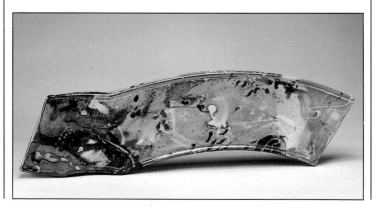

4 For hollow sections the clay must be reasonably soft, as the extruding process forms them in two halves, which rejoin as the clay leaves the die plate.

The lively surface decoration of John Glick's Extruded Form incorporates a variety of decorative treatments, including the multiple application of slips and glazes in conjunction with wax resist and painting.

FACETING

This decorative technique, involving cutting away vertical slices from cylindrical forms to produce facets, is normally associated with wheel-thrown pottery. The facets are either cut immediately after throwing or the form can be partly thrown and faceted before further throwing takes place. In either case the cylinder should be thrown with considerably thicker walls than normal so that after cutting there will still be sufficient thickness to prevent them from collapsing or tearing.

The facets are cut with a downward movement of a wire held taut between the fingers. The cylinder need not be removed from the wheelhead until faceting is completed. If a rounded form rather than straight cylinder is to be faceted, this should be done at the cylinder stage, after which the form can be swelled by applying pressure from the inside (see THROWING). Care must obviously be taken not to touch the decorative faceting on the outside of the pot in any further throwing or the effect will be lost. If sufficient clay is left above the faceted area, further throwing and shaping can be done. Where few facets are required the pot should be gently beaten (see BEATING) into the corresponding number of sides before they are cut.

Faceting can also be carried out on leather-hard pots, in which case a sharp, flexible blade rather than a cutting wire should be used.

1 Sections can be sliced off a thickly thrown form with a tautly held cutting wire immediately after, or even during, the throwing process.

2 Further shaping can take place after faceting as long as it is restricted to the inside or sections such as the rim, which have not been faceted. The outer surface will be spoiled if touched during subsequent throwing.

3 Where a limited number of facets is required, it is advisable to beat the thrown shape carefully into the desired number of sides before cutting, as this will prevent part of the wall being accidentally cut completely away.

4 Facets can be varied in width to good effect. Here, wide and narrower facets are being alternated.

5 The angular nature of faceted sections can be relied upon to produce an effective contrast to the natural, rounded qualities of a thrown form.

The sharp qualities of the cut sections on this thrown stoneware pot by Janet Leach create a pleasing contrast to the generally rounded shape.

FIRING

Firing is the process of applying controlled and sustained heat to clay or clay and glazes in some form of kiln. There are various types of firing, each of which produces different effects.

Bisque Firing

Bisque firing is the first stage, which transforms clay into permanent pottery. This usually precedes GLAZING. Whatever the kiln type or fuel used, the basic principles are the same. To minimize risk to the pottery, all items should be given sufficient time to be thoroughly dried out before firing. Where pieces of work are particularly thick, it is recommended to preheat the kiln to ensure that everything is as dry as possible. Articles to be bisque fired should be packed into the kiln as closely as possible: items can touch, rest on each other, be placed inside each other, or be stacked rim to rim or foot rim to foot rim.

Bisque firing will normally reach temperatures of anywhere between 1652° and 2012°F (900° and 1100°C) depending upon the type of clay used and the degree of porosity required – the higher the temperature, the lower the porosity. Clay manufacturers always offer recommended firing or "maturation" temperatures for particular clays. The initial stages of firing are the most critical as the "dry" clay still contains a high percentage of chemically combined water which turns to steam and must be allowed to escape slowly so that it does not force off sections from the walls of the pottery. The heat should be allowed to build up gradually inside the kiln until a temperature of at least 1112°F (600°C) has been reached, after which time the firing can proceed more quickly.

Modern technology offers the potter temperature control and monitoring equipment such as heat input regulators, pyrometers, thermocouples, and a host of sophisticated equipment which can be pre-set and programmed to increase temperature at a given rate, maintain or "soak" at set temperatures, and then to switch off at a particular time or temperature.

Enamel Firing

Enamels offer a spectacular color range to the potter, and are applied to the surface by mixing the pigment with a special medium prior to application. Enamels are also frequently screen-printed in the form of transfer designs. These are removed from their backing paper by soaking them in warm water and are then placed onto a pre-glazed surface and fired. Enamels are usually fired to between 1292° and 2012°F (700° and 900°C), some colors being able to withstand higher temperatures than others. The kiln needs to be of a sufficiently high temperature to melt the surface of the previously glazed surface without burning away the enamel pigment. The enamel decoration fuses permanently into the glazing.

Glaze Firing

This, also known as glost firing, is normally a second firing of pottery after bisque firing and GLAZING, and it fuses the glaze to the pot. The temperature required will be determined by the glaze and the clay body. The following temperature ranges are most commonly used.
Earthenware (including red/terracotta clays) 1652°–2012°F (900°–1100°C)
High-fired earthenware 2012°–2192°F (1100°–1200°C)
Stoneware and porcelain 2192°–2552°F (1200°– 1400°C)
Care is needed when packing a kiln for a glaze firing. Unlike in bisque firing, pots

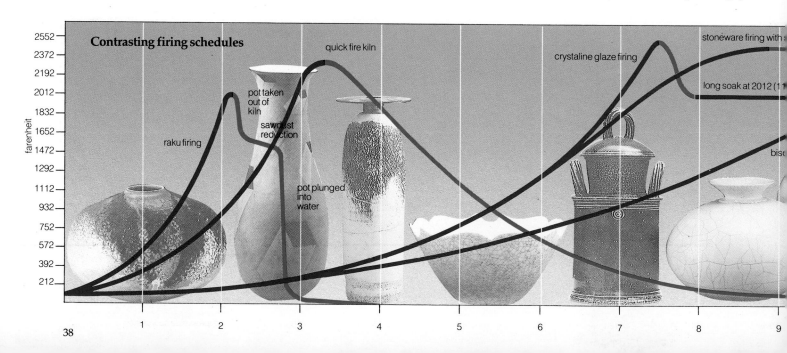

Contrasting firing schedules

quick fire kiln

stoneware firing with s

crystaline glaze firing

long soak at 2012 (1

raku firing

pot taken out of kiln

sawdust reduction

bis

pot plunged into water

farenheit

2552
2372
2192
2012
1832
1652
1472
1292
1112
932
752
572
392
212

1   2   3   4   5   6   7   8   9

should not come into contact with one another or they will stick together once the glaze melts. Bases of pots to be fired above earthenware temperatures should also be free of glaze or they will become firmly fixed to the kiln shelf. In earthenware firings "stilts" are used to stand pots on. These leave tiny sharp fragments embedded in the glaze which have to be carefully ground off.

Glaze firing can normally proceed at a faster rate than the initial bisque firing, although it should be slowed down as it reaches the required temperature so that the glaze can melt and "mature" properly. In raw glazing (see GLAZING), which cuts out the bisque-firing stage, the initial temperature rise should be slow until at least 1112°F (600°C), after which it can proceed as a normal glaze firing.

◄ Even moderate-sized kilns can accommodate a surprising number of items of varying sizes for a bisque firing, since pieces can touch one another without sticking together. Available space can be used to good effect by stacking similar items rim to rim (a process referred to as "boxing"), or by placing smaller items inside larger ones.

▼ Of the many stages through which the making of pottery goes, the firing process is arguably the most important. Until clay comes into contact with heat it will not be turned into pottery, but the types of firings clay can undergo are many and varied, resulting in different finishes. The rate at which a firing takes place also varies with the effects required and the type of kiln used.

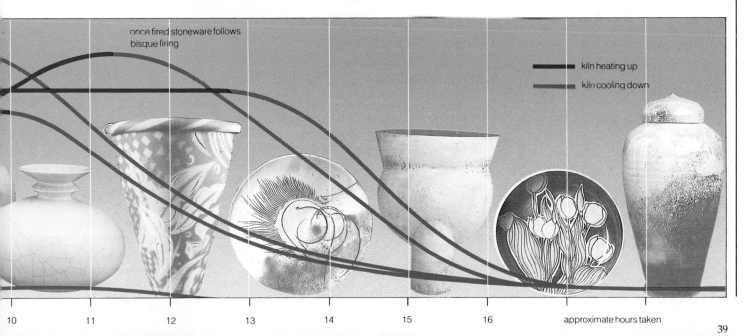

once fired stoneware follows bisque firing

kiln heating up

kiln cooling down

| 10 | 11 | 12 | 13 | 14 | 15 | 16 | approximate hours taken |

Crystalline Glazes

Large crystals can be encouraged to form in glazes containing zinc and titanium oxides, which act as the seed from which the crystals grow. The firing of crystalline glazes requires careful temperature control, involving rapidly heating the kiln to stoneware temperature so that the glaze becomes fluid (it is the glaze fluidity which determines the distribution of crystals on the pot) followed by rapid cooling to a temperature of approximately 2012°F (1100°C). This temperature is then maintained or "soaked" for anything up to five hours, during which time the crystals form. Because of the deliberate fluidity of crystalline glazes, adequate precaution needs to be taken to ensure that they do not run off the pot and fuse onto the kiln shelf. It is common practice to fire these pots on special bisque-fired saucers that serve to catch any glaze which runs off the pot. Excess glaze can then be ground off the pot base.

Oxidized Firing

The type of atmosphere within a kiln during the firing will affect the appearance of the pots. Electric kilns in which no burning takes place create an atmosphere with sufficient oxygen to allow complete combustion and to combine with the metals present in both clay and glaze. Because carbon dioxide gas is given off, this is described as an oxidizing atmosphere. Typical results from this type of kiln, which are quite different to those obtained in reduction firing (see below), include "clean" unspotted surfaces, colors from tan to dark brown obtained when iron oxide is used in glazes, and a variety of greens produced by using copper oxide or carbonate in glazes.

Reduction Firing

This is done in a kiln fired by combustible fuels such as gas, oil, wood, etc, where the supply of oxygen can be limited to prevent full combustion taking place. This will produce carbon monoxide which, if hot enough, will take oxygen from the metals present in both clay and glaze and produce totally different effects to those of an oxidized firing. Typical effects obtained by reduction firing include pronounced specks of iron bleeding through to the surface of the pot and through glazes; celadon glazes of pale blue and green which can be obtained by adding small percentages of iron oxide to a stoneware glaze; and deep reds such as the *sang-de-boeuf* glazes developed during the Chinese Ch'ing dynasty, obtainable by using copper oxide or carbonate in glazes.

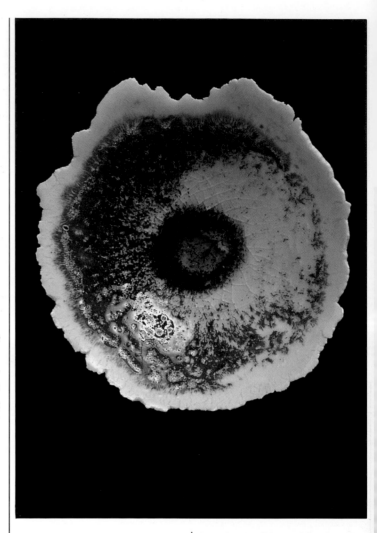

In reduction firings, "blood red" colors can be achieved by using copper oxide or carbonate in glazes, as in this piece by Jo Burton.

Preparing for glaze firing

1 This pot has been bisque-fired, and wax emulsion is now being painted on its foot rim to prevent any glaze from adhering to it.

2 Stilts of varying sizes can be purchased on which to stand pots during the glaze firing, necessary where the glaze covers the base. Stilts should only be used, however, at earthenware temperature, as they will collapse at a higher one. Care must also be taken to grind off any fragments of stilts which become embedded in the glazed surface, as they can be extremely sharp.

◀ Barbara Cass's rounded pot is a good example of the effect of a reduction firing on a clay body heavily laden with iron. The iron bleeds easily through the clay and glaze to produce the characteristic speckling, particularly pronounced in this piece.

▲ Precise temperature control is required during glaze firing to allow crystalline glazes to develop their spectacular effects. The large crystals in this porcelain pot by Elsie Blumer were achieved by a sustained period of several hours "soaking" after the initial stoneware temperature had been allowed to drop to below 2012°F (1100°C).

FLUTING

This is the technique of cutting decorative grooves into the clay surface. The grooves can be flat, concave, or convex in section, and are usually made with special fluting tools designed to allow the removed strip of clay to fall away after cutting. This technique is often found on thrown ware with the fluting contained within a band and formed vertically or at a slight angle rising from the foot to the rim of the pot. Among contemporary potters, the work of both David Leach and Lucie Rie often incorporates this technique as a decorative feature on bowl forms.

Fluting involves the careful cutting into the clay surface to create an edge of clay, and is most easily carried out on straight-sided pots or cylinders as these allow the grooves to be parallel and of uniform width from top to bottom. Rounded pots or those with the bases narrower than the rims are trickier to cut, as care has to be taken to allow for the swell in the shape. As in most techniques, sureness of purpose is important to the success of the final result. Practice can be gained by using a support to ensure a straight edge. On thrown pieces, fluting can be carried out almost immediately after throwing or left until the pot is soft-leather-dry. Straight-sided forms can be thrown, fluted and then shaped by swelling from within the form, as long as the outer side with the fluting is left untouched during the shaping (see FACETING).

1 A straight-sided thrown form can be fluted by drawing a suitable implement up a straight edge. Fluting is most effective when contained between a well-defined band or section.

2 If fluting is carried out while the pot is still attached to the wheelhead, further throwing and shaping can be done afterward. Any contact between hands and the pot, however, must be restricted to areas which have not been fluted, such as the inside or rim.

3 If sufficient clay remains at the top or rim area, further shaping can be done, or the height can be increased.

GLAZING

This is the process by which glaze (a thin coating of glass) is applied in liquid form to the porous surface of a bisque-fired pot before glaze firing (see FIRING).

Glazes consist of three main elements which are found in a variety of minerals containing silica, which produces the glass. The first is the silica, the second a source of flux, such as boron, which lowers the melting point of the silica, and the third a stabilizer which prevents the glaze from running off the pot when it melts in the glaze firing.

Glazes not only seal the porous clay so that it cannot be penetrated by liquid, they also offer limitless aesthetic potential. Glazes of incredible variety in color, surface quality, and firing temperature can be purchased in powder form from suppliers, but many potters who wish to have total control over their work prefer to make their own from raw minerals.

Applying Glaze

The following techniques can also be used to apply colored slips to the surface of pots before bisque firing (see SLIP DECORATION). Most methods of applying glazes to pottery, with the exception of DUSTING, require the glaze to be in a liquid state. The powdered ingredients are mixed with water, and the mixture is then sieved through a mesh size which can vary from only 40 up to 200 holes per square inch, depending on the fineness of glaze required.

Brushing glaze onto the surface of a pot can be an effective technique when the pot has already been given one or more coats of glaze: patterns and areas of different colored or textured glazes can be applied by brushing to produce rich surfaces. However, brushing as the sole means of glazing a pot is rarely successful as it is very difficult to produce an overall even surface. Matt glazes particularly will usually leave traces of brushstrokes on the surface after glaze firing.

If a sufficient quantity of glaze is available, the easiest method of applying it to the inside of the pot is to pour it in, whirl it around the inside, and then pour it out. The outside can then be coated by briefly immersing the pot in a bucket of glaze. If it has a sufficient foot rim to grip, it can then be held upside down to allow any droplets to fall until the surface of the glazed pot has lost its "wet look," at which point it can be handled carefully without spoiling.

Glaze can be applied to the outside of a pot by pouring, in which case the pot should be rotated slowly while this is done. This is a good method of applying several different glazes to one pot, as the different layers of glaze can produce attractive areas of contrast. If more than one glaze is poured, the first one should be allowed to lose its wetness before another is added.

To produce very even layers, glaze can be sprayed on. This should be done in a well-ventilated area in a spray booth with appropriate extraction facilities, and a face mask should be worn at all times as the inhalation of glaze particles is very dangerous. An advantage of spraying is that only small amounts of glaze are

Passing glaze through a sieve
Glazes can either be made by the potter to specific recipes using a variety of powdered materials, or they can be bought mixed in powder form. They are usually applied to pots in a liquid state, and when mixed with enough water to form a creamy consistency, the glaze should be passed through a sieve of approximately 100-mesh size.

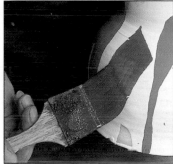

Applying decorative glaze
Although glazes can be brushed onto pottery surfaces, the result is likely to be uneven and patchy. Brushing is most effective when used to apply a second glaze covering over part of a glazed area as a means of adding a decorative feature.

needed. A spray gun and compressor are normally used, although small spray kits with disposable compressors are adequate for occasional spraying. Care should be taken to build up layers of glaze evenly or it will form puddles and run. The spray gun should be held about 18 in. (46cm) away from the pot's surface, and the pot should be rotated gradually to ensure overall coverage.

Coloring oxides and thinned slips can also be sprayed on. Airbrushes have become quite popular among potters in recent years, although these are used to spray finely ground colored ceramic pigment over areas of a pot's surface as decoration rather than as a means of glazing. Spray diffusers can be useful for spraying small amounts of thin glaze, oxides, or colors, but since they require considerable effort they are not suitable for large areas. Stiff bristle brushes or old toothbrushes can be used to spatter glaze, slips, or oxides onto surfaces (see SPATTERING).

Raw Glazing

This is the technique of combining the bisque firing and glaze firing (see FIRING) as one single process. Pots treated in this way are known as once-fired ware. Glazing can be done at any stage for this method, but it is usually carried out between leather-hard and dry. The glazes used can be applied in the same way as bisqueware or dusted on (see DUSTING). Not all are suitable for raw glazing, and experiments should be carried out in advance as some will flake off the pot during drying and firing. The inside of the ware should be glazed before the outside, with the process completed as quickly as possible and with great care as the water from the glaze will begin to soften the unfired clay walls.

Once glazing is completed, the pot must be left to dry out completely before being fired. The firing schedule for raw glazing should follow a similar pattern to a bisque firing, with a very slow rise in temperature until at least 1112°F (600°C) is reached. At this point a similar procedure to that outlined in glaze firing can be followed until the desired temperature is reached.

This detail taken from one of Walter Keeler's thrown, cut, and assembled jug forms is a good example of the typical "orange peel" surface texture characteristic of salt-glazed ware.

Salt Glazing

This technique, which involves introducing damp salt into the kiln at stoneware temperatures, is an old one which has gained renewed interest from potters all over the world. It is a process also used commercially to glaze drainage pipes.

When the damp salt is introduced into the hot chamber of the kiln, the sodium from it combines with the silica present in the clay to produce a glassy covering over the surface of the pots. In the process the inside of the kiln and kiln furniture also become salt glazed, and highly toxic hydrochloric acid fumes are given off into the atmosphere.

The surface color of salt-glazed ware is dependent upon the type of clay and any slips used. Pots which are to be salt glazed can be bisque fired first (see FIRING).

Salt glazing has been used extensively in Europe since the beginning of the sixteenth century. It is said to have been introduced by German potters who used the technique in the production of utilitarian wares. The first salt-glazed pieces had little in the way of additional decoration, but were later to be embellished with impressed decoration (see IMPRESSING). One of the most popular early examples of German salt-glazed ware is the bellarmine jar with its molded bearded face around the neck section, which was also copied in England by John Dwight.

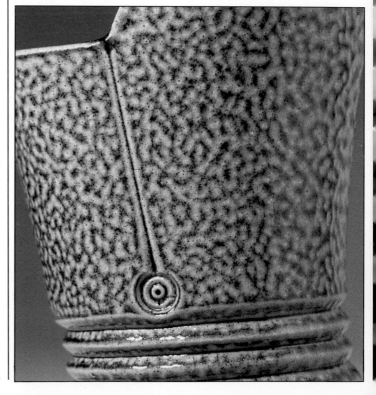

Methods for applying glaze
1 When possible, it is best to glaze the inside of pots first so that any spills onto the outer surface can be removed before the outside is glazed. Glaze can be poured inside, swirled around, and then poured out again, leaving an inner coating of glaze.

2 The whole pot can be immersed. If the pot is held level, air will be trapped inside, thus preventing glaze from reaching the inside. This allows you to apply one glaze on the inside by pouring, and a different one on the outside by dipping without the two mixing.

3 Glaze can be poured over a pot to cover either the whole surface or particular sections of it. Pouring glazes produces specific effects, which can be controlled with practice.

4 A number of different glazes can be overlapped to produce interesting decorative effects. However, care should be taken not to allow very thick areas to build up or the glazes may run during firing.

The functional yet highly individual saltware of Gus Mabelson displays a well-considered use of technique. His traditional shapes are nicely complemented by his very contemporary use of decoration.

IMPRESSING

One of the most natural and effective forms of decoration, and one used throughout all ages and cultures, is that of making marks by impressing objects into the clay surface. Any objects can be used for impressed decoration, and it is done while the clay is still soft enough to take the impressions without cracking or splitting, yet firm enough to give crisp definition. Clay can also be pressed or rolled onto textured materials such as rough woven textiles or netting, old terry bathtowels, or even aluminum foil to produce a variety of subtle patterned surfaces. These can then be used in decoration or in the actual construction of work (see SLABBING).

Custom-made texture stamps for impressing can be made easily from coils of clay of various widths. The flattened ends of the coils can themselves be impressed with pattern, and when bisque fired will remain quite durable. Such stamps can be used to produce embossed patterns by impressing them into soft applied clay on the surface of the pot.

This decorative form by Carol Jacobs, inspired by studies of small gardens, was produced by draping and wrapping a soft pliable clay sheet around a frame. The heavily impressed and incised surface was painted with a range of subtle, low-temperature colors, resulting in an effective ceramic patchwork.

1 A variety of tools and improvised objects can be useful for impressing decorative patterns into soft clay.

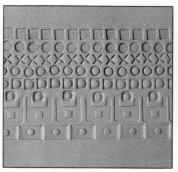

2 Organized bands or layers of patterns can be built up using very simple shapes, which produce rich textural patterns.

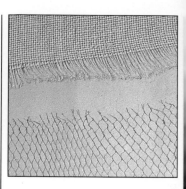

3 Coarse open-weave fabrics and netting can be rolled or pressed into the clay to leave interesting surfaces.

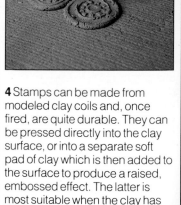

4 Stamps can be made from modeled clay coils and, once fired, are quite durable. They can be pressed directly into the clay surface, or into a separate soft pad of clay which is then added to the surface to produce a raised, embossed effect. The latter is most suitable when the clay has hardened.

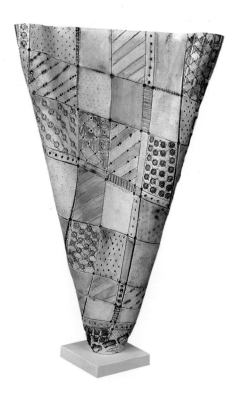

INCISING

Incised decoration is that made by cutting into the clay surface. The type of tool used and the dryness of the surface will determine the quality and definition of the cut edge. Lines cut into wet clay with a pointed instrument will produce very immediate designs with burrs along the edges, while incising a leather-hard surface with a sharp blade will produce very precise edges. In either case the most effective designs will be those which are unhesitant and flowing, as are some of the fine examples of this technique seen in the Chinese porcelains of the T'ang and Sung periods.

On leather-hard or dry but unfired pottery the design can be drawn out roughly on the pot before beginning to cut. This can be done freehand, or previously drawn designs can be transferred by tracing them through carbon paper, which will leave a line to follow on the surface.

Traditionally, incised decoration is covered with a pale-colored but transparent celadon type glaze (see FIRING), which gives the work a pleasing surface and also accentuates the layered decoration beneath. Coloring oxides can be rubbed into the decoration to accentuate the design further prior to glazing.

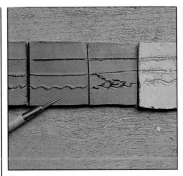

1 The quality and definition of the cut or incised line is determined by the tool used and the state of dryness of the clay. These four slabs of clay show the same line cut into clay surfaces which vary from soft (left) to bone dry (right). Notice how the shaving pares off cleanly leather-hard, but is reduced to dust at the bone-dry stage.

3 Leather-hard clay can be incised with a sharp blade, which will leave a crisp, well-defined edge. In order not to blur or damage the cut edge, shavings and clay fragments should be removed carefully with a stiff brush.

5 For incising bone-dry clay surfaces, a sharp scalpel is the ideal tool. Pots in this state are extremely fragile so great care must be taken to prevent accidental chipping or cracking.

2 Although the most flowing and fluid incised decoration results from working freehand, this may initially seem a little daunting. Where the clay surface is soft or leather-hard, designs can be traced on by drawing over the design. This provides an effective guide in the form of a slightly indented line.

4 Tracing paper backed with a sheet of carbon paper can be used to transfer a design onto a dry clay surface. This leaves a dark line which is easy to follow.

Peter Lane's porcelain bowl has an intricately incised surface. The addition of a small percentage of copper carbonate to the glaze produces a light green tinge which enhances the delicate pattern.

INLAY

Attractive decorative effects can be made by filling cut or impressed recesses in the clay surface with clay of a different color. This technique, usually referred to as inlay, mishima, or marquetry, was used widely in the decoration of English medieval tiles.

The recesses can be thin lines or larger areas dug out of the leather-hard surface. The shrinkage rate of the inlaid clay should be the same as that of the pot, or cracks will appear in the design as the two clays separate. One way of ensuring that this does not occur is to use only one base clay and add coloring stains in much the same way as clay is prepared for AGATEWARE.

Where colored slips are used for the inlay, as in the Japanese mishima technique which uses contrasting black and white, the slip is best left until very sticky before use. A fine grog can be added to slips used for inlay in order to reduce shrinkage (see ADDITIVES). Many medieval tiles were made by flooding carved recessed surfaces with contrasting-colored slips, which were scraped back when leather-hard to reveal the decorative contrasts.

An alternative form of inlay decoration can be used by preparing thin colored clay motifs which are then laid down on a suitable surface and moistened slightly. A sheet of soft clay is then placed on top and rolled gently with a rolling pin. The motifs will sink into the clay surface which can then be used to form a slabbed pot (see SLABBING) or used in a mold to shape (see JIGGER AND JOLLY, PRESS MOLDING, SLIP CASTING).

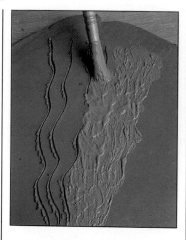

Inlaying with colored slips
1 Inlaying can be done by filling incised lines with thick colored slips. The risk of the slip shrinking and causing cracking can be reduced by adding fine grog.

2 When the lines have been filled, the slip is left until the surface has stiffened. Once leather-hard it can be scraped with a flexible smoothing tool or other suitable object, removing the surplus slip and revealing the thin lines of color.

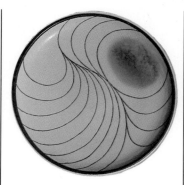

Inlaying black lines in a light-colored clay is a traditional Japanese technique called mishima, used on Harrison McIntosh's thrown stoneware bowl, to produce precise black lines as a balance to the solid area of green.

Inlaying with colored clays
1 Here defined pattern areas have been dug from a leather-hard surface into which colored clays are to be inlaid. The dug out areas are scored and dampened to assist adhesion of the clay.

2 The colored clays are then pressed firmly into place, with some surplus above the surface. The inlay is left to stiffen before any attempt is made to tidy the pattern.

3 Once the clay has stiffened sufficiently to be scraped, a suitable blade or flexible steel object can be used to reveal the precise inlaid decoration.

2 The colored clay motifs are taken up into the clay surface to become embedded or inlaid into it.

Inlaying with ready-cut motifs
1 Motifs in contrasting-colored clays have been cut from very thin slabs of clay and laid out over a porous surface. A slab of soft clay is then placed over the motifs and rolled.

3 The inlaid slab of clay can then be formed over a suitable mold. In this instance, a hump mold is being used, so that the inlaid surface becomes the inside of the shallow rectangular dish.

The effective surface decoration of this elliptical stoneware vase by Jo Connell was achieved by inlaying decorative motifs made from a range of pastel-colored clays.

JIGGER AND JOLLY

Pottery can be formed in rotating plaster molds with the use of a mechanical arm to which a metal-profiled template is attached. When the mold forms the inside shape and the profile the outer surface, the process is referred to as jiggering, while the reverse, with the mold forming the outside shape, is called jollying. In both processes, the molds fit into a "cup wheelhead" to hold them in place.

Sabina Teuteberg is a potter who uses the potential of this technique to good effect in the production of individually decorated tableware.

Jiggering is normally used to form plates or shallow dishes. A slab of plastic clay is placed onto the convex shape of the mold, and while it rotates, the mechanical arm with its shaped metal profile is lowered onto it. The profile is lubricated with a little water and the arm is preset to be lowered only to the point at which the correct thickness of clay is achieved over the mold.

Jollying is most frequently employed in the production of deep shapes such as cups (minus handle which is normally made by SLIP CASTING) or cylinders, the shapes being limited to those that can be easily removed without snagging in the mold. A prepared lump of clay is placed in the bottom of the concave mold and can be roughly spread up the walls by hand as the mold rotates. The jolly arm with the profile is then lowered into the mold to complete the spreading of the clay to form the required internal shape and attain an even thickness.

1 Here Sabina Teuteberg combines forming and decoration techniques to produce very individual pieces. Although it is not essential to use clays of more than one color for the jigger and jolly process, she creates bold patterns by organizing thin sections of contrasting-colored clays onto a prepared slab of plastic clay.

2 Interesting effects can be achieved by combining clays of contrasting colors (see AGATEWARE). Here, thin coils are incorporated into a main base-colored clay. This can then be compacted by rolling, as you would an ordinary coil of clay, and can be cut into thin sections or strips for use.

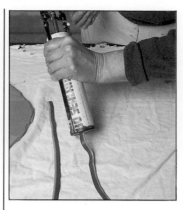

3 Pleasing color combinations can be achieved by extruding clays of two or more different colors. The random effect will produce subtle variations with each extrusion. Here, a simple extruder which can be purchased from most hardware stores is used to good effect.

4 This detail of the patterned clay slab shows quite clearly the raised level of the colored sections which were laid onto it.

5 The contrasting-colored clay patterns are embedded into the clay slab by rolling. For small quantities of clay, a rolling pin is adequate for this kind of work, but here a large, hand-operated bench roller is used to bed in the design.

6 Sufficient pressure has been applied to ensure that the pattern is embedded into the slab without destroying or distorting the crispness of the design.

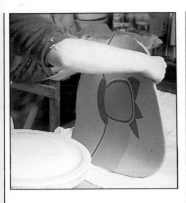

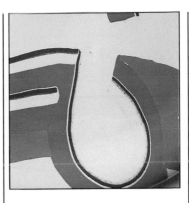

7 The decorated sheet of soft, pliable clay is now ready to be placed onto the convex surface of the plaster mold.

9 The profile template on the jigger arm is then slowly brought down onto the rotating clay to define the required outer surface shape of the plate. The excess clay builds up around the template as it is lowered to the pre-set level.

11 Before the newly formed plate is removed from the plaster mold, any form of decoration suitable to the soft plastic state can be carried out. Here, colored slip is banded over the surface.

12 Crispness and sureness of pattern definition on the inside of the plate is maintained during the jigger process. As the photograph shows, this side is directly next to the plaster surface, and is not touched by the shaping profile.

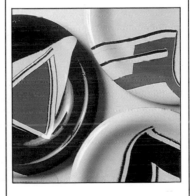

8 When the mold has been secured into the specially designed wheelhead, known as a "cuphead," the slab is pressed down, initially by hand, as the wheelhead rotates.

10 Excess clay is trimmed away from the edge of the mold with a knife before the template is brought down again to give the shape a final definition.

These decorative and functional plates by Sabina Teuteberg have been created by inlaying colored clays, resulting in powerful, graphic surface patterning which reflects the popular trend towards bold and simple imagery.

13 Jollying defines the inside of a deep-sided shape with the profile, while the outside is in direct contact with the plaster mold. In order to prevent the large, pliable clay slab from creasing as it is placed into the deep recess, it is being laid in two sections.

14 As in jiggering, the initial pressing down of the clay sheet into the mold is done by hand as the mold rotates, securely held by the cuphead.

15 Initial excess clay is trimmed away with a knife before the inside template is lowered into bowl.

16 The profile shape is lowered to the required pre-set level, thus forming the inside section of the bowl to the desired thickness.

17 Once the inside shaping is complete, decoration can be applied to the inner surface. Here a dark-colored slip is being brushed on. The bowl will be left to stiffen before removal from the mold.

18 Literally hundreds of working molds can be cast from a single solid-plaster "master." A large number of molds is necessary for the jigger or jolly process, as work cannot be removed immediately after completion. This master cup mold is coated with a soap solution to seal the plaster surface before a metal collar is positioned to create a containing wall around it.

19 Liquid plaster is then carefully poured into the metal collar until the original mold is totally covered. The freshly poured plaster is left until it has set.

20 Once this new working mold has dried out thoroughly (which will take several days), it is ready for use. Note the row of similar working molds on the back shelves.

KNEADING

Before clay is used it must be prepared to ensure it is of an even consistency, contains no air pockets or foreign bodies, and is in the appropriate state of wetness or dryness for the techniques that are to be employed. Even prepared clay bought in a plastic state will require a little further preparation before use as it soon loses its even consistency and will be wetter in some parts of the bag than others. Clay stored outside in plastic bags for any length of time will also need further preparation, particularly if it has stood through cold weather, as frost will have frozen the water content and broken down the clay structure and initial even consistency.

Clay manufacturers use a large pug mill to prepare clay for use. Clay is fed into a hopper and forced into a large barrel where it is mixed by slowly rotating angled fins before it is compressed and extruded as a thick solid section. When a pug mill is not available potters use the method of kneading combined with WEDGING.

Kneading is done while the clay is soft but not sticky. Use an absorbent surface such as a wooden work bench or a plaster slab which will absorb some of the water content. If plaster is used it must be in good condition or pieces could be taken up into the clay.

Gather the clay into a compact mass and press down onto it with the palms of your hands, pushing it away from you at the same time, then raise it from its back and repeat the sequence in a smooth rocking motion. As the developing roll of clay lengthens it can be given a quarter turn and repeated. An alternative method of kneading is to apply downward pressure with one hand while lifting the mass from the work surface with the other in a rhythmic, flowing action, resulting in a spiral pattern. At this stage ADDITIVES in a variety of forms can be blended into the clay by slicing it into layers and adding the material in between successive layers which should then be kneaded together.

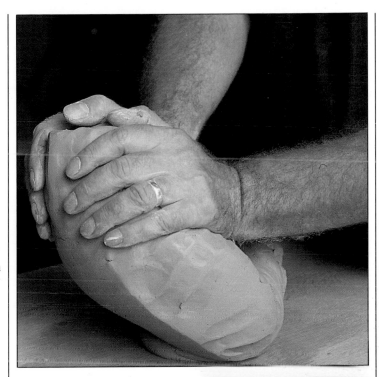

1 Clay is kneaded to prepare it before use. Apply downward pressure with the palms of your hands, pushing the clay away from you.

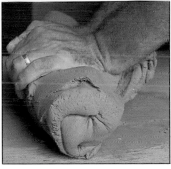

2 The kneading process should be carried out several times to ensure that the whole clay mass is thoroughly mixed.

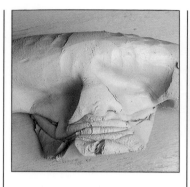

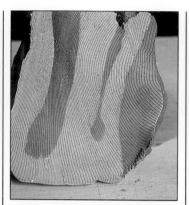

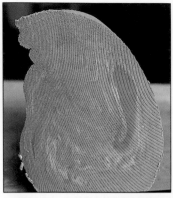

3 This form of kneading gives the clay mass its characteristic shape.

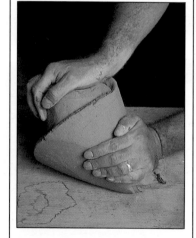

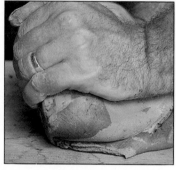

4 Bearing down on the clay mass with one hand only while steadying it with the other can be an easier way to knead large quantities. This method is usually referred to as spiral kneading.

5, 6 Kneading is a good way of blending together two or more different-colored clays. Alternating layers are slapped together and then kneaded to mix and blend them.

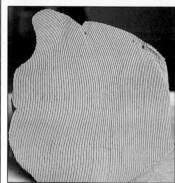

7, 8, 9, 10 These sections sliced through two contrasting-colored clays during kneading show how the blending takes place. Initially the clays are easily identifiable as separate colors. After some kneading, the characteristic agate patterning develops, while further kneading begins to break down the color distinctions until the two clays are inseparably blended.

LIDS AND FITTINGS

Lids are normally made by the SLIP CASTING or THROWING techniques. The best lids form natural relationships with the body of the pot, and they rely on one another to produce a successful unified whole. Lids should thus always be considered during the initial DESIGNING process, and thrown lids should be made at the same time as the pot. This also helps to ensure a good fit as both will shrink at the same rate.

Although lids can vary widely in shape, form, and function, there are really only a few main types on which all others are based. All lids require some device to keep them securely in place, and this is usually achieved through forming and combining flanges and galleries. These tend to define the different lid types.

Simple inset lids can be formed by throwing totally enclosed shapes. These can be cut through with a sharp blade in an undulating line when leather-hard, or alternately formed with an integral flange during throwing and cut to fit when leather-dry. Another type of lid is a simple cup or bowl shape which caps the rim when inverted over it. A well-defined ledge for the cup lid to rest on is normally a feature of this type. Similar lids can rest on internal galleries formed on the pot.

Where the rim of a pot does not have a gallery, the lid will require a flange which fits into the throat of the pot. This type can be thrown as an inverted shape and have a handle attached at a later stage (see PULLING), or alternately can be thrown upright with a solid or hollow knob handle formed during the throwing process. Flanged lids are also frequently thrown for pots with internal galleries to ensure a close fit.

This smoked and lustered ginger jar by Gerry Unsworth shows an effective use of a simple cup or cap lid fitting over the throat of a jar.

Simple variations on lids and fittings

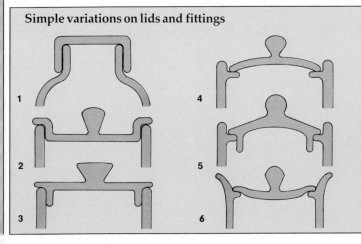

1 A simple "cup" lid fits snugly over the throat of the pot. 2 This lid can be easily thrown incorporating the knob during the throwing stage. It can be used where the maximum width of the pot is required. 3 This lid can be used on pots with or without internal galleries. 4 A simple flangeless lid sits on an internal pot gallery. 5 A flanged lid combined with an internal gallery is commonly used in articles where a secure fit is required to enable pouring/tipping and so on, as in the teapot. 6 This lid is a simpler version of style number 2.

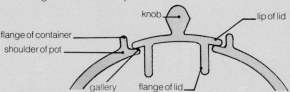

knob
lip of lid
flange of container
shoulder of pot
gallery
flange of lid

Making a simple lid

1 The simplest form of lid is nothing more than a small bowl or dish shape which, when inverted, forms a cover or cap. Such lids can either fit over and enclose a rim or they can sit on a formed gallery inside the rim.

3 Here the flange is given sharpness and definition with a tool held at a 90° angle, with the underside of the lid supported with the fingers.

4 Lids thrown in an inverted position will normally require some form of knob or handle. This can be a section of pulled or extruded handle, but an alternative is to throw a small knob directly onto the lid. Center the lid in an upright position on the wheelhead and fasten it securely with soft clay. Score and attach a small ball of clay to the lid. Use slurry to ensure a good bond between knob and lid surface.

5 Using the minimum amount of water, throw the knob shape from the soft ball of applied clay.

2 To make a flange on a simple lid, begin by compressing the rim to thicken it. Determine where the flange will form and split the resulting thickened rim with your fingernail. Press down steadily on the split section.

This robustly thrown casserole by Seth Cardew features a well-fitting lid whose pleasing domed shape echoes that of the body of the pot. The casserole features cobalt brush decoration over a white stoneware glaze, and has been wood-fired.

Making an integrated knob

1 Lids thrown right way up can incorporate a knob. Open out the clay, starting slightly off the exact center so that as you push down you form a small peak in the middle of the clay.

3 The knob can either be left solid or hollowed by pushing your thumb into it. The base edge can be trimmed to produce a sharp edge before the lid is removed from the wheel.

Making a gallery for a lid

1 Many pots need securely fitting lids. This can be achieved by forming an internal gallery for the lid. Compress the rim to thicken it by applying downward pressure with the index finger of one hand while supporting the rim with the thumb and index finger of the other.

3 A suitable implement which gives a 90° angle can be used to define the internal gallery.

2 Open the clay out to the required width, allowing it to grow over the edge of your finger, which supports it underneath.

2 Define and split the thickened rim with your fingernail, and begin to depress the inner section to make the gallery, supporting it as it forms.

MAJOLICA

This is the anglicized term for *maiolica*, the white tin-glazed decorative earthenware which had its roots in the medieval Islamic world, but began to be made extensively in Italy during the fifteenth and sixteenth centuries. Italian maiolica has since been an important influence on the decorative wares of Europe. The techniques employed are similar to those of faience from France, fayence from Germany, and delftware from Holland.

Majolica is a form of in-glaze decoration (see also COLORING and DRAWING). The surface of the pottery is traditionally covered with an opaque white tin glaze, and the pottery can be either previously bisque fired or raw glazed (see FIRING and GLAZING). Potters now use a variety of glazes which produce similar results to the original tin glazes, but the basic techniques are similar. Colored pigments are painted onto the white glaze surface before glaze firing (see FIRING), during which the colors sink only slightly into the surface, leaving the decoration permanently fixed and clearly defined.

Italian maiolica developed into a distinctive narrative form of decoration: the white surfaces were treated by artists of the time as canvases onto which were painted scenes of contemporary life or episodes from myths and legends. Modern potters often decorate the white glazed surfaces, using techniques such as the painting on of color with specialist pottery brushes, sometimes in combination with colored pigment applied by methods such as sponging.

Using a brush
1 White tin-glazed surfaces lend themselves well to decorative brushstrokes. Lining brushes are useful for painting thin lines which may serve as outlines to further areas of color and decoration.

Using a sponge
Color can be applied to the glazed surface with a sponge, which will add texture as well.

Using other materials
Patterns can be stamped into a glazed surface with an open-weave material. Such patterns can either be used as a background or as a means of filling in defined areas.

2 Broad flat brushes can be used to place color into the glaze. Brushmarks can vary from thin lines to thick, solid areas, depending on how the brush is held.

Daphne Carnegy used oxides and commercial stains applied over an earthenware tin glaze to produce the in-glaze majolica decoration on this bowl. Surface areas are defined by painted outlines into which color was applied by brush and sponge.

MOCHA WARE

This is a distinctive type of pottery with moss, fern, or tree-like surface decoration, achieved by applying a liquid containing tobacco and coloring oxide to a freshly slipped surface. The "mocha tea," as it is known, reacts with the wet slip to produce organic patterns which remain clearly defined when the pottery is fired. The name of the ware comes from its resemblance to the Arabian quartz, mocha stone. It has been produced in England from 1785, although it only became well established as a commercial technique in the Staffordshire potteries in the nineteenth century, when it was commonly used in the production of jugs and mugs for taverns.

1 Before the "mocha tea" can be applied, the leather-hard pot is coated with slip. Where sufficient quantities of slip are available, dipping is recommended, as this will produce a thick, even covering.

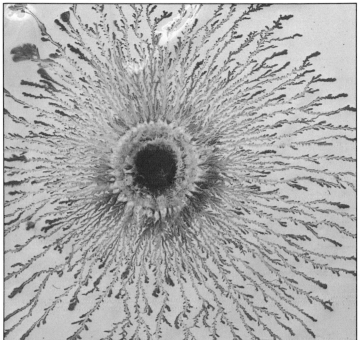

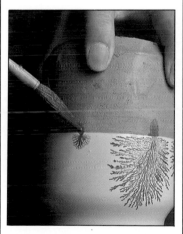

2 While the slipped surface is still quite wet, the pot is inverted and the edge of the slipped band touched with a laden brush of the mixture. As if by magic, a tree-like design emerges, which will continue to grow while the slip remains wet if further tea is applied.

3 Flat surfaces can also be treated with mocha tea. Here mocha tea is dripped through a slip trailer onto the freshly slipped surface of a tile. A fern-like pattern is produced, which radiates from the point of application.

4 This detail of the tile shows the delicate structure of the pattern, with the "eye," the point at which the tea was applied, clearly defined.

PIERCED DECORATION

Cutting through or piercing holes in the walls of pots and dishes is a form of decoration that has been used since as far back as the twelfth century in Persia, and it is thought that it developed from the popular fashion of piercing in silversmithing. In the Chinese Ming Dynasty, piercing pottery was referred to as "devil's work," for although an effective form of decoration, it increases the danger of breakages and takes both time and patience to complete.

Once clay has become leather-hard it is in a suitable condition to be pierced. A sharp blade or suitable hole-boring tool should be used, and since the piece of work is weakened considerably by piercing, care should be taken not to make the holes too close together. The outside of the form should be supported throughout the operation. Piercing often leaves very sharp edges, which can be softened by the careful use of a damp sponge unless this is an effect particularly required. An alternative is to clean up the pierced areas with steel wool once the clay has dried sufficiently, but this is a more hazardous process and could result in breakages.

For repeating or stylized designs, TEMPLATES can be used to draw in the shapes to be pierced.

Tiny pierced holes will fill up when glazed and produce a pleasant translucent effect, used in twelfth-century Persia in an effort to imitate the translucency of the Chinese Sung porcelains.

1 A collection of sharp-bladed tools and hole-boring implements is required for successful pierced decoration.

2 Clay should be left until leather-hard before piercing and cutting out, and care must be taken to support the work while it takes place. Areas to be removed can be planned in advance and outlined with a needle or pin. Sharp edges can be removed with a blade, or carefully smoothed with a damp sponge when piercing is complete.

3 Tools specially made for boring are readily available in different sizes from suppliers. It is always worth remembering that the more clay is removed, the weaker the structure becomes, with a commensurate increase in the likelihood of damage.

This porcelain bowl with a diameter of about 10in (25.5cm) displays a masterful use of piercing. Peter Lane's pattern is based upon the observation of the spaces in hedges, and his bowl successfully conveys an impression of interweaving branches and treetrunks.

PINCHING

This is one of the simplest and most direct of hand-forming pottery techniques, and provides a valuable introduction to working with clay. Any clay is suitable provided it is soft and pliable but not sticky. A variety of subtly different pinched shapes can be produced which vary from tall thin shapes to shallow open forms, each produced by gently rotating the ball of clay in one hand while the thumb and fingers of the other hand thin and shape the walls. The wall should develop with an even thickness, and a foot can be formed either by rolling the base along an edge to define it or by adding on a thin strip of clay to form a small cylinder for the pinched form to stand on.

The rims of pinched forms can develop in an undulating and uneven manner. This is entirely appropriate to a technique often used for work inspired by natural or organic forms, as in that of Mary Rogers and Alan Wallwork. However, a level rim can be obtained if required by carefully trimming the rim edge with a sharp knife or pin.

Small spheres can be produced by joining two similar sized small bowls together rim to rim.

1 To begin a pinch pot, hold a small ball of soft clay in one hand and insert the thumb of your other hand into the middle. Push your thumb down to about ¼in. (5mm.) from the bottom and start to gently squeeze the clay between thumb and fingers, slowly rotating the clay ball.

3 A base can be attached to the basic pinched shape. Here a thin strip of clay, rolled out and cut to size, has been attached with slurry. The seam is then welded together with a modeling tool to ensure a good joint.

2 Shapes that widen too much can be narrowed by making folds in the wall and welding them together with your thumb and fingers. The increased thickness of clay can then be used to increase the height.

2 As the wall thins, move your fingers up towards the rim. Pinching should be done slowly so that the form evolves gradually with an even thickness throughout the clay wall. The rim can be thinned and allowed to flare outward as a natural progression of the shape. Undulating rims are well suited to delicately pinched forms.

Making a narrow pot
1 A narrow, pinched shape can be made by first pulling the clay up over your thumb and then pinching the shape between thumb and fingers while the clay is slowly rotated.

3 Pay attention to the top section and rim. Careful thinning at the rim can be a delicate operation. The base can be teased out to form a slender stem, but this must be stable enough to support the completed form. It is sometimes necessary to sit the form in a container to support it until the clay has stiffened sufficiently to take the weight. Further refinement of the shape can be made by cutting and scraping at the leather-hard stage.

PRESS MOLDING

Plaster molds are used when a potter wants to produce complex forms that are difficult to achieve by hand-forming methods, or needs to make a large quantity of identical objects. These have been in common use since the eighteenth century. Clay items can be made from molds by SLIP CASTING, press molding or the JIGGER AND JOLLY technique.

Press molding involves pressing sheets or pellets of soft, pliable clay into or over the surface of the mold, and is a popular method of making shallow dishes or simple forms. Single molds with a concave surface are generally referred to as "drop" molds, since the clay is pressed or dropped into them. Those with a convex surface are known as "hump" or "drape" molds because the clay is draped over the plaster form.

Two-piece molds can also be used, in which case each piece of the mold is pressed separately. The edges are then scored, slurry is added, and the two pieces are locked together to form the final shape.

Simple use of a drop mold
1 Laying soft pliable sheets of clay into a plaster "drop" mold is a simple but effective way of making shallow dishes.

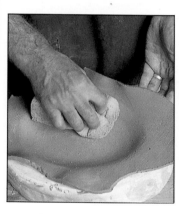

2 The clay sheet is carefully eased into the plaster mold with the help of a dampened sponge.

3 A wet flexible rubber tool is used for final shaping and smoothing of the inside surface of the dish.

4 Surplus clay is removed from the edge of the dish by pulling a tautly held wire along the plaster surface. Surface decoration can be applied to the dish while it is still in the mold, and then left to stiffen until dry enough to handle.

Surfaces of simple, shallow press-molded dishes offer enormous potential for highly decorative surfaces. John Ablitt has used a variety of different colored slips to produce the precise geometric design on his burnished dish. It has much in common with textile patterning.

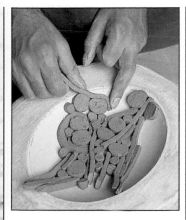

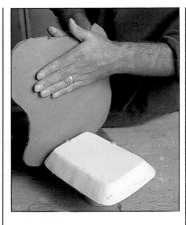

Exploring the decorative potential of drop molds
1 Hollow forms with rich, textural outer surfaces can be made by joining together two similar press-molded sides. A two-piece mold is ideal for this, although a single one can yield the same result, as shown here. Begin by covering the inside of the mold with individually shaped pieces of soft clay to a depth of ¼in (5mm).

3 Leave the second half in the mold, score and apply slurry to the edges of both halves, and press the two together. The hollow form can now be worked on further by creating a foot or neck. Or it can be left as it is, with nothing more than a small hole at the neck and a flattening of the base to enable it to stand upright.

Using a hump mold
1 Dishes can be formed by draping soft pliable clay sheets over "hump" or "drape" molds.

3 The outer surface of a hump mold can be covered with small clay shapes, which, when smoothed together, will produce a shallow dish with a highly textured interior.

2 Once the mold surface is covered, blend the pieces of clay together to ensure a strong bonding of the separate shapes. If large molds are being used, it is advisable to thumb in extra clay to form a thicker section. Carefully turn out this first half onto a suitable board and make the second half in exactly the same way.

Jo Connell uses press molding to create her highly decorative vessels. The patterns are inlaid into the surface of the clay sheet before being press-molded, with the inlaid surface facing the mold. The two sides are made separately.

2 The sheet of clay is eased over the mold using a damp sponge to assist shaping, and the excess clay is then trimmed away with a wire or other tool to define the rim of the dish.

4 The textured interior can be left as it is or made more functional by filling the spaces with a clay or slip of contrasting color. When this is scraped down, the contrasting colors will accentuate the clay pattern shapes as well as providing a smooth filled surface.

PULLING

Clay sections are often "pulled" in order to produce handles and other attachments for pots. These can also be formed by other processes such as EXTRUSION or SLIP CASTING, but pulled handles are particularly appropriate on thrown ware.

To pull a section, first shape a well-prepared (see KNEADING and WEDGING) piece of clay of a size comfortable to hold into a rough carrot shape. Hold this with your left hand (or right if you are left-handed) and, while lubricating the clay with water, tease the shape gradually downwards, thinning and increasing its length as you do so with the thumb and index finger of your working hand. As the length of the pulled section increases, it can be flattened by additional pulling with thumb and index fingers held parallel. Before completion, a thumb groove can be formed by dragging the thumb tip down the pulled length. Once the section is pulled to the desired length and thickness, it should be left to stiffen slightly before being attached as a handle or lug.

An alternative method is to attach a section of clay to the side of a pot first and then pull it in much the same way so that the handle is formed directly on the pot.

The clay should be reasonably soft for pulling and well lubricated. This minimizes the danger of fingers dragging and causing fractures to develop in the length through uneven pressures. Pulled sections can be kept very simple or made more elaborate by twisting or patterning before use.

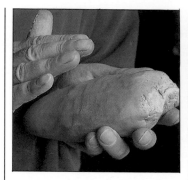

Pulling a handle separately
1 Before pulling begins, a well prepared piece is patted into a thick carrot shape which can be held comfortably.

2 With hand and clay both well lubricated, the clay is teased in a downward movement. The pressure must be gradually and evenly applied along the full length of the clay, or weaknesses will develop which will lead to it breaking. Once sufficient length has been pulled and the handle is the required thickness, a thumb groove can be added by drawing the thumb steadily down the center of the clay.

Pulling a handle directly from the vessel
1 The piece of prepared clay is shaped and attached firmly to the side of the pot or jug, using stiff slurry to ensure a good bond.

2 The handle is then pulled normally, but with care taken not to damage the jug. It is important to ensure that the handle springs from the correct position and is aligned with the spout.

3 Once the section of handle has been pulled, the unattached end is joined equally firmly to the side of the jug. Care needs to be taken over positioning, so that the top and bottom of the handle are correctly aligned. Once attached, the handle joint can be smoothed with a damp sponge.

4 The finished qualities of pulled handles complement thrown pieces extremely well. There should always be a visible element of tension in any pulled handle shape.

RAKU

Raku ware was developed in sixteenth-century Japan as a low-fired form of pottery. The pots, usually small bowl-like forms, were glazed and used for Japanese tea ceremonies.

The immediacy of the raku firing method, which involves removing the ware from the kiln while red hot, and its attractive surface qualities have vastly increased its popularity with Western potters during the past decade. The violent and rapid changes in heat that the ware must be subjected to requires a special open body which contains a high percentage of grog or sand (see ADDITIVES). This can be made up by individual potters, but many excellent raku clays are available from pottery suppliers.

Raku pottery can be made by any forming method or a combination of techniques. Thin-sectioned forms are generally more successful and any joints are particularly vulnerable to cracking during the firing and consequent cooling. Where clay sections have been joined together during the building process, special care should be taken to ensure these are welded together properly (see SLABBING). The pots can be decorated in much the same way as other forms of pottery during the appropriate stages of drying and firing, and they should be bisque fired as normal, but to approximately 1652°F (900°C) to ensure they are very porous and able to withstand severe thermal shock. After bisque firing the pots can be glazed using any suitable method (see GLAZING) with raku glazes and colorants, and glazes should mature between approximately 1652° and 1832°F (900° and 1000°C). They can be purchased from suppliers ready for use, or are easily made from a variety of available frits to which about 5–10% of clay should be added with metallic oxides for color.

Raku Glaze Firing

Theoretically, any type of kiln can be used for a raku glaze firing, but in practical terms, the fact that metal tongs are used to extract the hot ware from the kiln makes electric kilns potentially dangerous unless the current is first isolated. Considerable amounts of steam and smoke can be given off as part of the process, so the firing should take place in the open.

The kiln temperature is raised up to approximately 1832°F (1000°C) and the glazed pots are placed somewhere warm (usually the kiln roof or around the sides) to remove the water from the glaze. The dried pots are then placed into the glowing kiln chamber with tongs, and left in the kiln until the glaze surface appears "wet," indicating that the glaze has melted. This stage may take anything from 5 to 20 minutes, depending upon the type of kiln and glazes used.

Once the glaze has melted, the pots are removed and while still hot can be covered in sawdust or other combustible organic materials such as dried leaves so that reduction (see FIRING) takes place. Crackle glazes are a feature of the raku process, and if this effect is required the pots should be exposed to cold air for a few moments before covering, as this will encourage crackling. After the pot has been covered (some potters leave them for only a few minutes, while others allow them to cool completely in dampened sawdust for an hour or more) it is then immersed in water to complete the cooling process. This also prevents the glazed surface of the pot from re-oxidizing. Particularly delicate or enclosed forms should be left to cool gradually in damp sawdust rather than in water as this cuts down the risk of breakages. When cooled, pots should be washed and cleaned with steel wool or a suitable alternative to reveal the full surface colors.

1 Here glazed pots have been placed around the kiln so that they can dry out thoroughly before being fired. Do not worry if some smoke discoloration occurs, as this will not affect the final results.

2 Glazed pots can either be placed inside the kiln and allowed to heat up with it, or they can be put into the kiln chamber with long metal tongs when it has reached approximately 1832°F (1000°C). If no accurate means of indicating temperature is available, estimate that this heat will have been reached when the chamber glows bright red.

4 After removal from the kiln, the pot is placed in a lidded metal trashcan containing sawdust or other combustible material, covered with the same material, and the lid replaced. Because the supply of oxygen is limited, reduction will take place, dramatically altering colors and surfaces. For example, slips or glazes containing copper will turn deep bronze and red, while any unglazed parts of the body will turn black.

6 The reduction effect is fixed by plunging the flaming pot into water to cool it rapidly. It is at this point that the pot is most severely tested; poorly made joints or thick sections may split or crack open. Any pieces which are enclosed or particularly fragile are best left to cool slowly by covering them in dampened sawdust after reduction.

3 A careful look into the chamber will indicate when the glazes have melted, at which point they are ready for removal. Try not to open the door too often or heat loss will occur, and the glazes will take longer to reach melting, or "maturation," point. The pots are ready when the glaze covering looks wet, as can be seen in this photograph.

5 Exposure to air as the pot is removed from the sawdust will cause it to burst into flames and begin to re-oxidize, lightening the body and reversing the colors back to their oxidized state.

This small group of thrown and altered raku pots by the author was glazed using a combination of white and green glazes. The firing chamber was just large enough to house all four at once, and they were removed in rapid succession. The heavy reduction has caused the green copper-bearing glaze to turn deep bronze and the raku clay body to blacken where it remained unglazed.

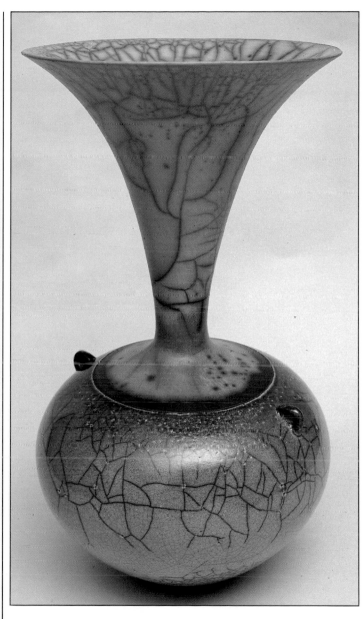

▼ The brightly glazed swirling fish design on Frank Boyden's enclosed thrown form, Carp Vase, contrasts with the black reduced areas. These were treated with *terra sigillata* slip to produce the velvet-smooth surface.

▲ This elegant coil-built raku bottle form by David Roberts shows a heavily crazed glazed surface. He encourages this effect to develop by leaving the pot in the open air for some minutes after removal from the kiln before reducing it. The reduction then blackens the lines and creates rich surface patterning.

▲ A combination of slips, stains, multiple raku firings, and sandblasting have all been used by Harvey Sadow to produce the iridescent coloring of this vessel.

RESIST DECORATION

A variety of materials and media can be used to mask off areas of a surface to create decorative effects. The form of resist chosen will make its own contribution to the decoration, and can be combined with other decorative techniques. Wax, paper, and a variety of other materials have been traditionally used for resist work, although in recent years more sophisticated masking fluids, latex, and glues have gained popularity.

In general, resists can be used at any stage during the pottery process, but some forms are more appropriate to particular stages. While the clay surface is still in a plastic state, paper can be cut or torn into shapes and used as a simple but effective form of resist for colored slips. Wax emulsion can also be used to resist slip, although the slip should not be too thick or the resist will not work (see SLIP DECORATION). After bisque firing (see FIRING), wax emulsion, latex, and glues can be brushed, trailed, or dribbled onto the surface and allowed to set before colorants or glazes are applied (see COLORING and GLAZING). Such resists can be left to burn away during the subsequent firing or, in the case of latex and glue, carefully peeled off before firing, with further resist decoration built up. These techniques can also be used on freshly glazed surfaces, with additional glazes or color applied over the top prior to the firing.

Paper resist patterns
1 Slightly dampened paper forms a simple yet extremely effective method of resist for colored slips. Simple or quite complex shapes can be cut or torn from paper, which should be slightly absorbent so that it adheres to the plastic or leather-hard surface of the clay. Slip can be applied over the resist in a variety of ways, including spraying, pouring, and brushing.

2 Once the surface of the slip has lost its wet shine and can be touched lightly without marking, the paper resist can be removed with a needle or pin. Here an uneven soft edge is given by tearing rather than cutting the paper.

For her delightful Cockerel Pizza Plate, Josie Walter used paper resist to mask off the main decorative areas, after which further colored slips were infilled by trailing and brush decoration. The dish is red earthenware clay, raw glazed in an electric kiln.

Wax resist patterns
1 Liquid wax emulsion can be painted onto glazed surfaces, to form a resist. Brushes should be washed thoroughly in hot water and a little detergent to remove wax from the bristles.

Wax resist forms an important part of Peter Beard's technique. He applies the resist patterns with brushes or patterned sponges to the glazed surface, and builds further layers of glaze on top. The dry glaze used gives an attractive, highly textural quality to his work.

2 The wax, once dry, repels any further glazes or water-based colorants, and can be used as an effective means of creating patterned surfaces.

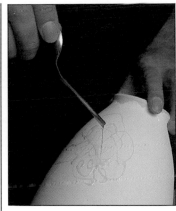

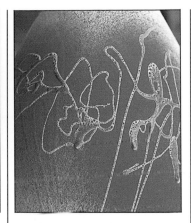

Using latex glues

I Latex glues are gaining popularity as resist mediums. Thick areas of a glazed surface can be masked off with these glues. And when the glue is dry, a second glaze or color can be applied over the first one. Here iron oxide is being spattered onto the surface of a pot with an old toothbrush.

2 When dry, the latex is peeled off, leaving a clearly masked area free from the spattered iron oxide. This area can now be decorated further with additional glazes or color. Potters often employ lively, complex patterning in masked areas to create pleasing contrasts.

3 The viscosity of some glues allows them to be trailed freely across glazed surfaces, leaving a very distinctive free pattern.

4 Further glazes or oxides can be applied when the glue has dried. Here a mouth-diffusing spray is used to apply iron oxide to the glazed surface.

5 This detail of the glue resist shows the tiny droplets of iron-oxide-colored water collecting on the surface of the dry glue. To retain this attractive effect, the glue need not be peeled off. If left on the surface of the pot to burn away during firing, the droplets of iron oxide remain, creating interesting textures.

The surface of this pot by the author was trailed with a mixture of glue and a dark brown slip. The linear pattern was then covered with a matt white stoneware glaze and fired in an electric kiln. The brown slip content of the glue resist has bled through the surface of the white glaze to produce the striping.

ROLLED DECORATION

Repeated marks and patterns can be made in the surface of soft or plastic clay by using simple textured rollers or roulettes. Patterns can be carved into the surface of plaster, wood, and other materials or alternately simply carved or impressed (see IMPRESSING) into soft coils of clay of varying thicknesses. These can be bisque fired when dry, and remain permanently usable.

Rolled impressed decoration can be used to very good effect in producing patterned sheets of clay which can then be used in SLABBING. Texture rollers can either be simply rolled over the clay surface with the palm of the hand or makeshift handles can be formed from stiff wire such as coat hangers.

Roulettes have since early times been a popular means of achieving narrow bands of textured pattern on the outsides of freshly thrown ware, and the technique is still much used on ware of a functional nature today.

Rollers made from sponge or similar flexible and absorbent material can be used to apply banded areas of coloring oxide decoration onto freshly glazed surfaces prior to glaze firing; patterns can also be lifted out from freshly slipped or glazed surfaces with sponge rollers (see STAMPING/STIPPLING).

1 A variety of textured rollers can be made by rolling soft clay coils over textured materials. When dry, these can be fired to form permanent texture rollers.

2 Bisque-fired rollers can be impressed into sheets of soft clay to produce textured slabs, which in turn can be used to construct a variety of slabbed forms.

3 Narrow roulettes are an effective means of impressing bands of texture and pattern into the surface of newly thrown pots.

SGRAFFITO

This is the term used for scratching or incising through a colored slip or glaze to reveal a different color underneath. It is one of the most common and most widespread decorative techniques, found in all ages and cultures, and although extremely easy, it has the potential for producing extremely intricate and varied effects.

Sgraffito designs can be scratched through colored slip while still wet, or left until the surface is leather-hard or even bone-dry. The quality of the scratched line will be different at each stage of dryness. Intricate designs can be lightly drawn first on a leather-hard or very dry surface with a pointed tool, or they can be traced on over a carbon backing.

Designs can also be made on surfaces for raw glazing (see GLAZING), immediately after the glaze has been applied, when the body of the pot is softened by the water content of the glaze. A pot which has previously been bisque fired is less suitable as it is difficult to incise lines through the glaze without areas flaking off.

Fired glazed surfaces can be successfully reglazed with a second contrasting glaze through which a sgraffito design can be scratched. In order to help the second glaze to adhere to the first, it is sometimes necessary to warm the pot before application, particularly with stoneware pieces where the body is no longer porous. Spraying (see GLAZING) is a particularly useful method of applying a second glaze.

1 The state of dryness of the slipped clay surface will determine the quality of the line produced by the sgraffito technique. A wet clay surface will produce a clearly defined line, but the burrs thrown up in the process will adhere to the line and be difficult to remove if not required as part of the effect.

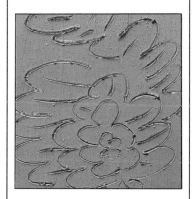

2 At the leather-hard stage, sgraffito lines can be scratched through easily with a minimum of burrs.

3 When the slipped surface has reached the bone-dry state, sgraffito lines throw up dust. This should be cleared away carefully with a stiff bristle brush so the lines are not obscured.

Jenny Clarke's stoneware teapot shows a simple but effective use of the sgraffito technique. Her subtle color was achieved by glazing the slipped decoration with matt white, which reduced the strength of color in the iron-bearing slips she used.

4 Sgraffito is usually associated with slip-covered clay surfaces, but it can also be done on glazed surfaces. When a contrasting-colored second glaze is applied, scratching through the second surface will reveal the first. If a second glaze does not adhere easily to the previously glazed surface, warming the pot first will help it to do so.

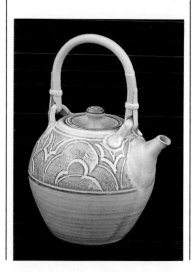

SLABBING

Sheets or slabs used to form pottery objects offer large surfaces that give the potter considerable potential as they lend themselves to virtually every decorative technique.

Slabs can be rolled individually, with the clay placed on a piece of burlap or other fabric to prevent it from sticking to the work surface. A rolling pin is used in conjunction with wooden rails to ensure an even thickness. The slab should be turned regularly, and rolling should take place from the center outward, allowing the clay sheet to spread more easily.

Slabs can also be cut directly from a block of clay using a cutting wire, or can even be extruded (see EXTRUSION). As large slabs are particularly prone to warping during drying and firing, coarse clays with a high grog and sand content are advisable.

The clay slabs cannot support themselves when soft and pliable, and are best formed around or into MOLDS or formers which can in turn be used as part of a further construction or forming technique. Cylinders can be formed simply by wrapping a pliable clay sheet around a tube or rolling pin, which should first be covered in newspaper to enable easy removal.

If left until leather-hard, clay slabs can be cut and joined, and TEMPLATES of stiff cardboard or simple paper used to ensure uniform shapes and sizes. Clay slabs to be joined should be carefully scored and stiff slurry applied, with additional reinforcement provided by a clay coil blended into the joint.

Cutting slabs

1 Cutting wire is used to cut slabs of clay of even thickness directly from a prepared block. After each slab is cut and removed, the wire is moved down a notch.

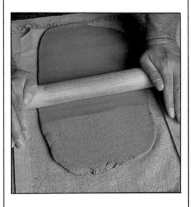

2 The slabs are then rolled out with a rolling pin on fabric, using guides to obtain an overall even thickness. Begin rolling from the center of the clay, as this will enable it to spread across the fabric without becoming too embedded. Turn the clay sheet regularly.

Making a cylinder

1 To make a slabbed or wrapped cylinder, begin by cutting off the ragged edges at the top and bottom of the clay sheet. Wrap newspaper around a section of tubing and form the clay sheet around it. The fabric on which the clay was rolled can be used to assist you.

2 Overlap the excess length of clay, and then cut through both layers at an angle of 45°. Remove both offcuts. Score both edges, apply stiff slurry to the scored areas, and slot the two edges together to form a tight seal.

3 A base can be added by scoring and slurrying the edge of the cylinder base and the proposed clay base. The section of tubing can remain in place until the clay begins to dry out; shrinkage will trap the mold, making it impossible to remove.

4 Any unevenness (unless a planned feature) can now be removed. Measure and mark the lowest point of height around the rim, then join up these points to form the line along which the rim should be cut. If possible, a soft, thin coil should be applied and blended into the joining seam. The cylinder can then be decorated or used to form part of a more complex piece of work.

▶ The black and white patterns on this slabbed pot by Michael Bayley are very thin slices taken from a block of laminated clays. These slices were laid out on a slab of clay and rolled into the surface, after which the inlaid clay was allowed to stiffen before being assembled.

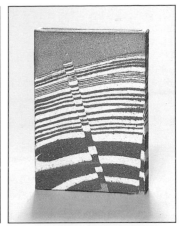

Making a box shape

1 Leather-hard sections can be joined together to create slabbed work, in which case each side must be carefully scored and slurried first. Work on top of the base where feasible, and reinforce each joint with a thin, soft coil welded into successive joints.

3 Once all the sides are joined, outer joints can be smoothed down with a suitable tool. They should also be carefully welded together on the outer surface to reduce the risk of splitting.

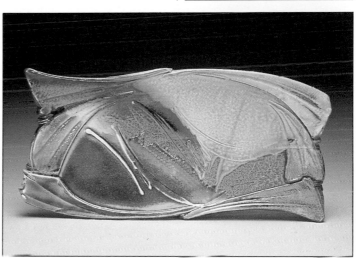

▲ The rounded contours of this slabbed tray by Steven Hill are reminiscent of the Art Nouveau style. The impressed and slip-trailed surface treatment and multiple glaze applications combine to create a highly decorative yet functional object.

2 Using clay when it is in its barely flexible leather-hard state produces a crispness and formality of shape characteristic of many slabbed forms. It is advisable to use a coarse, open-bodied clay for this type of work, due to the pressures placed on the joints during drying and firing.

4 The rim can be measured and leveled in the way described in step 4 (opposite), using a sharp knife or small wire.

SLIP CASTING

This is a common industrial production technique whose popularity with studio potters has increased in recent years. It is an efficient and low-cost method that enables them to create mass-produced items that nevertheless maintain an individual character through their individual decoration. Casting slip is very different to that used for decoration, which is thinned only with water, as it contains an ingredient called a "deflocculent" (typically sodium silicate), which efficiently breaks the clay down into a liquid with the minimum of water.

The slip is poured into a plaster mold of one or more pieces depending upon the complexity of the object. Molds of two or more pieces are held together with thick elastic bands or string to prevent separation when filled, and a thin layer of pliable clay is deposited evenly over the wall of the mold. The porous plaster mold absorbs the water from the slip, so that the slip level drops gradually and needs to be refilled until the correct thickness of clay has been achieved. Any surplus is then poured out and the mold is left inverted to drain. When it stops, it should be turned upright and left until the deposited clay lining loses its shiny, wet surface.

Slip-cast items can be decorated in much the same way as any others, although casting normally produces thinner-walled items than other techniques, and this can make them less able to absorb the water content of glazes after bisque firing.

1 Specially prepared casting slip is poured into a two-piece mold, which is held together with thick elastic bands or string to prevent the pieces from separating. The mold will need refilling with casting slip, as some of the slip's water content will be absorbed by the plaster mold.

2 Once a thickness of about ¼in. (3mm.) is seen around the opening, the remaining slip is poured out. This must be done carefully, or a vacuum may form within the mold and bring the wet form away from the sides.

3 The mold is left inverted to drain. Feeling inside the pouring area with a finger will reveal whether the slip has dried sufficiently for the mold to be opened.

4 Any waste must be cut away carefully before the mold can be opened up.

5 The mold is then opened. Notice the locating pins which ensure the pieces fit tightly together in the correct position.

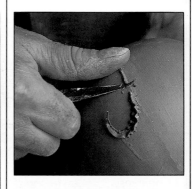

6 When the clay lining or cast can be touched without leaving an imprint, it is removed from the mold. Any surplus clay which has formed around the mold seam can be cut away, or "fettled," with a knife.

SLIP DECORATION

Colored slips, or "engobes," are one of the simplest means of achieving both color and decoration on unfired pottery surfaces. Slips can be applied in a variety of ways (see BANDING, GLAZING, STAMPING, SPATTERING) as well as by the methods of trailing, feathering, spotting, and marbling which are traditionally associated with slip decoration. Slip is often applied to surfaces which are to be burnished in order to achieve a color change from that used for the pot's body (see BURNISHING). Articles of pottery with slip decoration are normally referred to as slipware. Fine examples are to be found among the work of seventeenth-century Staffordshire potters such as Simson, Meir, and Thomas Toft.

Slips are clays in a liquid state with the addition of colorants in the form of metal oxides or coloring stains developed from them. They can vary in thickness for application, but as a rough guide, to cover the clay body, slip should be at least the consistency of cream unless a thin application is particularly desirable.

Many forms of decoration involve the use of slips in combination with other techniques, but those methods described here are traditionally used alone.

Slip Trailing

This is a method of drawing onto pottery surfaces using a slip trailer, a container with a nozzle. The technique is very similar to that of icing a cake: the clay surface is first coated with a layer of slip, and while still wet, slips of contrasting color are trailed onto it.

Feathering

Where contrasting-colored slips are trailed in parallel lines, one color can be partly pulled into another at a 90-degree angle to break the uniformity of the lines. The traditional tool for this was the tip of a feather, but a pin or needle will produce good results. Care should be taken to prevent the tool from catching on the surface of the clay underneath or the crispness of pattern will be destroyed.

Marbling

Areas of two or more contrasting-colored slips can be freely applied to a surface and then shaken sharply. They will then mix and form random marbled patterns, no one of which will ever be exactly the same as another.

Spotting

Patterns or pictures in slip can be built up by dipping the end of a piece of wood or metal into slip and then placing it on leather-hard clay. Spotting can also be done with a slip trailer, which can produce droplets of slip as well as an unbroken trail. In this case, the best effects are produced when a coat of wet slip is first applied over the whole surface so that the contrasting-colored spots sink into it.

When the slip decoration is finished it is left to dry, after which it is usually raw glazed or bisque fired and glaze fired.

Tube Lining

This is a means of defining decorative areas in a manner similar to slip trailing, which are then filled with color. It is usually done when the clay surface is in the leather-hard state. Slip made from the same clay as the pot is trailed to outline decorative areas, and after bisque firing the trailed lines, although identical in color to the rest of the surface, will be slightly raised. The areas defined by the raised lines are then colored with oxides or other underglaze pigments (see COLORING). A transparent glaze is applied over the top of the color, or alternately the pot can be glazed first and have the color applied over it before glaze firing as in the MAJOLICA technique.

Tube lining can also be done after bisque firing, in which case a glaze-like mixture rather than slip is trailed onto the surface, and further glazes are then brushed or trailed into the defined areas.

A thrown and fluted, raw-glazed (once fired) stoneware platter by Steven Hill. To achieve his rich combination of surface quality and sumptuous color, Hill combined impressed decoration and slip trailing beneath a number of glazes.

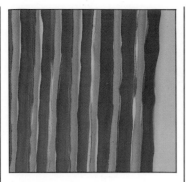

1 Slip trailing at its most simple consists of single lines of colored slip laid into a wet base slip. Alternating bands of different colored slips or criss-crossing lines can also be used.

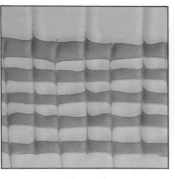

2 In feathering, a traditional slip-decorating technique, one colored slip is dragged through another with the tip of a feather or needle.

4 Colored slip can be spotted into wet slipped surfaces.

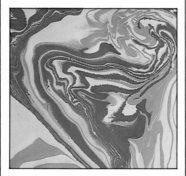

3 A strong marbling effect can be achieved by applying two or more different colored slips to a surface and then mixing them with a single, swift movement.

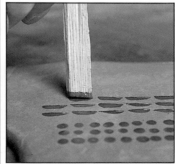

5 Spotting colored slips into an unslipped surface, a form of stamping, is a technique most commonly found in peasant pottery in parts of Europe.

The highly decorative surface of this stoneware basket called Amphitrite, by John Gibson, incorporates traditional slip decoration techniques such as trailing with areas of underglaze painting. Slips and underglaze colors were applied while the clay was still in a plastic state.

SMOKING (SAWDUST FIRING)

Smoking is a means of darkening pottery surfaces from a light gray to black in a uniform or random manner. The surfaces of low-fired articles lend themselves most readily to smoking; the smoke is less able to penetrate the surface of high-fired wares.

The process can be carried out simply by lighting tapers of paper underneath the pot, but the deep black layer of carbon this leaves on the surface will mostly wash away with water, so that only very pale traces remain. More durable results are given by building a small chimney of bricks around the pot or pots, filled with sawdust, shavings, shredded paper, or a combination. For an overall darkening, the pots should be well covered, but if patchy areas of smoking are required, parts of the pots are exposed. Set light to the surface of the sawdust or other materials with newspaper and allow the sawdust to burn down around the pots slowly, thus ensuring that the gray-black coloring penetrates the surface and remains permanent.

Pots can also be bisque fired in this manner, although they will be very fragile since the temperature is unlikely to exceed 1292°F (700°C). For a simple bisque firing it is vital to use only fine sawdust, as shavings and shredded paper will burn too quickly and cause the pots to shatter.

Smoking as a decorative technique is most commonly used with pottery which has been through a bisque firing (see FIRING). The smoked effect can be totally removed by refiring the pot in a kiln other than a sawdust-fired one.

1 Light smoking of a bisque-fired surface can be achieved by holding a lighted taper near to the pot, a method which allows controlled smoking of selected areas. The problem with the taper method of smoking is that it only makes a carbon deposit on the surface, and once washed, no more than a pale coloring will remain.

2 For a deeper, more permanent smoking of the surface it is better to build a small kiln around the pot made from ordinary bricks, with sawdust poured in carefully around the pot. If a variegated effect is required, patches of the sawdust can be brushed away from the surface in some areas.

3 The top of the sawdust kiln is then lit with a taper. The flames quickly die down to a slow smolder as the sawdust burns from the top downward.

4 When the sawdust has burnt down completely, the pot is removed and cleaned to remove any loose ash and carbon deposits. The blackened smoked surface will now be quite permanent, as the smoke will have penetrated the surface. If the final effect is unpleasant, however, it can easily be removed by giving the pot a second bisque firing, which cleans the surface.

This tall thrown bottle by the author was slipped and burnished before a glue resist decoration was trailed over the surface. After a light smoking, the glue was peeled away to reveal the linear pattern.

SPATTERING

Color can be applied to the clay surface in either its fired or unfired state in the form of a coarse spray. This form of decoration was used in mid-nineteenth-century England on some glazed earthenware which is generally known as spatter ware.

Although a spray gun or airbrush can be used for the spattering technique, there are a number of less sophisticated methods which are well worth trying, and in some instances give the potter more direct control over the process.

A stiff-bristled paint brush or an old toothbrush can be used to spatter colored slips or other colors by simply flicking the loaded bristles. A mouth-diffusing spray is ideal for applying colorants such as oxides, although care must be taken to stir the mixture frequently to prevent the oxides from settling to the bottom of the container during spraying. Slips or glazes, unless applied very thinly, are too heavy to be sprayed in this way.

Spattering color onto surfaces produces interesting results when combined with RESIST DECORATION.

1 Colors and slips can be spattered onto surfaces in a controlled manner by using stiff bristle brushes. Old toothbrushes are the perfect – and inexpensive – tool for this technique.

2 When only small areas are to be spattered, a mouth-diffuser spray can be an effective means of applying coloring oxide mixtures.

Blue slip was brushed over the surface of this tall thrown bottle before further pastel-colored slips were applied by spattering with an old toothbrush. The author then burnished the surface before it was bisque fired. Spattering the slips allowed careful control to be exercised over the patterning of the surface areas.

SPOUTS

Some pots require spouts for purely functional reasons, while in other cases they may be an aesthetic requirement. In either case, a common rule of thumb is to make additional component parts for any object by the same method of construction throughout. A thrown teapot, for example, will normally be best with a thrown spout, while a slip-cast spout is most suitable for a slip-cast teapot. However, rules are to some extent made to be broken, an example being thrown additions to slabbed forms, which can provide an exciting contrast of techniques that often adds to the success of the work.

In any form which requires additional components, great care should be taken to ensure that the proportional balance of the piece is correct when all the components are assembled.

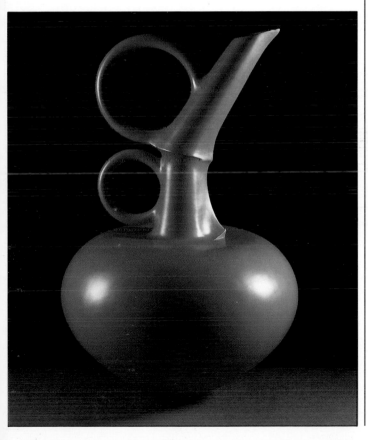

◄ The spout on this coiled and burnished non-functional pot by Magdalene Odundo is an aesthetic rather than practical requirement. It grows simply from within the form, beautifully poised, and balanced by the use of the two ring handles. Odundo's masterful control enables her to create forms of breathtaking precision with no loss of character or spirit.

▲ The immediacy of the throwing method encourages a fluid quality such as that seen in Steven Hill's splendid thrown teapot. The spout has been seen not only as an essential functional requirement, but also as a carefully considered part of the overall shape and design in relation to body, lid, and handle.

SPRIGG DECORATION

This term refers to repetitive clay motifs in low relief applied to a clay surface to form a decorative band or overall pattern, a technique also known as sprigging. The pattern is either first modeled in clay and then cast in plaster to form a simple mold, or carved in negative directly into plaster. Pliable clay is pressed into the mold and lifted out with a wet metal spatula or a small piece of clay. The resulting motif or sprigg is then fixed to the surface of the pot, using thin slurry or slip as the adhesive.

Clay of a contrasting color can be used to make the sprigg pattern distinctive, a technique well known to anyone who is familiar with the Wedgwood jasperwares. However, the same clay should be used for both body and spriggs, or the sprigging may crack away from the surface during drying or firing; if a contrast is required it is best to color some of the same clay body (see COLORING).

1 A negative mold of a decorative motif can be made by carving into the surface of a small piece of plaster.

2 The tiny carved plaster mold can be filled by pressing in a small piece of soft plastic clay with a finger.

3 In order to keep the press-molded motif as thin and delicate as possible, any excess thickness of clay can be trimmed off with a taut wire or, as here, a small "potter's harp." The clay motif is raised from the plaster mold by pressing firmly with a metal blade.

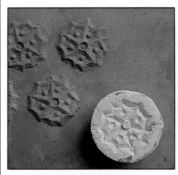

4 Sprigg molds enable repetitive clay motifs and shapes to be made. When these are applied to leather-hard clay surfaces with a little slurry, interesting patterns can be created.

5 At the Wedgwood factory thousands of sprigg molds are cast with slip. When the slip has dried enough to handle, the motifs are applied to the surface of leather-hard ware.

This group of sprigg-decorated Wedgwood Prestige Jasperware shows the blue-, green-, and black-colored bodies with their contrasting white sprigged surface decoration. This is perhaps the best known of the many decorative techniques employed by the Wedgwood potteries.

STACK THROWING/REPETITION

Although the use of industrial or semi-industrial techniques employing the use of PRESS MOLDING, JIGGER AND JOLLY, and even EXTRUSION are commonly employed to produce large numbers of similar items of pottery, the THROWING method can be used to produce a number of very similar if not identical forms. This requires considerable skill and expertise, often the result of years of practice. However, there are several basic tips which assist the potter. One of these is the careful weighing out and preparing of balls of clay before throwing commences, while another is using guides, gauges, or even profile-shaped TEMPLATES to pinpoint important heights or points of alterations in shape.

Where a number of small, simple shapes are required, a large piece of clay can be centered and items can be thrown in succession, taking only the top section of centered clay each time. This technique is called stack throwing.

1 Several small items can be thrown from a single piece of centered clay. Here, a small lid is being made, with throwing confined to the top of the clay.

2 A needle is used to cut into the center of the clay at the lid base while the clay rotates. The lid is then carefully lifted off.

3 Further lids can then be thrown from the remaining clay without the need for recentering between each one.

STAMPING/STIPPLING

The use of stamps made from a hard or durable material to indent or impress the surface of pliable clay is a simple and effective surface treatment (see IMPRESSING), but stamps can also be made from soft, absorbent materials, such as synthetic foam or sponge. The effect these create is quite different, as they will not only indent or impress the clay surface but will absorb colorants. If colors, particularly in the form of slips (engobes), are applied to a leather-hard surface, and patterned sponge stamps are then pressed into them while still wet, they will lift off part of the slip, leaving a patterned impression. This technique can also be employed with a glazed surface, although on a bisque-fired pot the glaze dries quickly unless it has had a high bisque firing (see FIRING) which has made it less porous. Stippling, the build-up of areas of textured colors, is simply achieved using a piece of sponge or other suitable material.

Stamping and stippling can be used as decorative techniques in their own right or in combination with a variety of other forms of decoration. In MAJOLICA decoration, for example, areas are often outlined with brush lines of various colors and thicknesses and then filled in with stippled color. Both stamping and stippling can also be used in conjunction with stencils and other forms of RESIST DECORATION.

1 Sponges will always produce their own distinctive patterns when used to apply color onto clay or freshly glazed surfaces. They can also be cut into intricate patterns which can then be transferred onto clay. Synthetic sponges like this common household one are easiest to cut – with scissors or a scalpel – if frozen first.

2 When dipped in colored slip, the sponge can be used to lay or "stamp" pattern onto leather-hard clay surfaces. Single, double, or multiple patterns, as here, can be made quickly and easily.

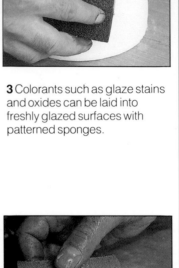

3 Colorants such as glaze stains and oxides can be laid into freshly glazed surfaces with patterned sponges.

4 A dry sponge stamp can also be used on wet, freshly slipped or glazed surfaces. This creates areas of patterning by lifting out rather than laying in, and produces delicate yet well-defined effects.

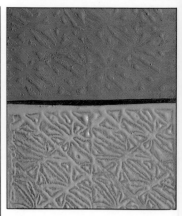

5 The top peach-colored slip pattern is substantially different in character from the lower white slipped section. The same piece of textured sponge was used in both cases, but the top pattern was made by dipping it into slip, while the bottom one is the result of lifting out from fresh white slip with the dry sponge.

TEXTURING CLAY

There is no such thing as a right or wrong texture for clay: some pieces of pottery may need to have smooth, easily washable surfaces for practical reasons, while a pitted or rough, dry surface might be well suited to a different piece of work. It is the function of the piece of pottery which determines its most appropriate surface, a factor which should be carefully considered during the DESIGNING process.

The body textures of clays vary enormously in their natural states. Some are smooth while others feel coarse or gritty, and these body characteristics affect not only the handling qualities and suitability for certain uses, but also the final fired surface appearance. A variety of materials, permanent and combustible (see ADDITIVES) can be introduced into the clay body to modify or change its texture, to make the body more "open," or to alter its handling characteristics.

A whole variety of decorative techniques can be employed to treat the clay at any time from its wet state up to bisque firing, and even after this stage the surface texture can still be altered quite dramatically by the application of glazes whose ingredients react with one another in particular ways at specific temperatures. Depending on the ingredients, the surface textures of glazes can vary from mirror-smooth and shiny to the typical silky matt of those containing the mineral dolomite or the rough volcanic surfaces which result if silicon carbide is added to a glaze in too great a quantity.

▲ The coarse-bodied clay used by Hans Coper for this thrown composite pot is clearly evident. The sculptural qualities of the piece have been enhanced by rubbing manganese dioxide into the unglazed clay, thus emphasizing its textured surface.

◄ Surface textures varying from mirror-smooth and shiny to volcanic and heavily pitted can all be achieved through the use of glazes. The textured and pitted surface of this stoneware bowl by Lucie Rie is the result of the introduction of silicon carbide into the glaze, which causes it to erupt and produce a lava-like surface.

▼ The author used black slip forced through a fabric mesh to build up the textured surfaces of these thrown and modified shapes. Stiff white slip was also scumbled over the top of the coarse crank-clay body to add contrast to the darkened areas.

TEMPLATES

Templates can be used at various stages during both forming and decorating processes in order to produce particular effects or shapes of a predetermined nature. In COILING, a template will ensure that the profile of a vessel grows to a required shape, while in SLABBING, it enables slabs of a similar shape and size to be cut before assembly. Extruded shapes or sections (see EXTRUSION) are determined by templates through which the clay is forced, and they can also have an application to THROWING when pots of a particular shape and size are required. The template or "profile" is used to form the inside or outside of the form in the JIGGER AND JOLLY process. But perhaps the most common use of templates is in techniques such as PIERCED DECORATION, where a pattern can be first drawn before being pierced or cut away, or in RESIST DECORATION, where paper stencils (a form of template) are used to inhibit the flow of slip, color, or glaze from specific areas.

1 Coiled shapes can be built up to a predetermined profile with the use of a template. As the pot grows, its shape is checked against that of the template. A simple cardboard template will normally suffice for once-only pieces, although if the same shape needs to be repeated, a more durable material should be used, such as wood or hardboard.

2 Paper or cardboard templates are often employed in slabbing, where several clay slabs of similar dimensions are required.

3 Stencils, a type of template, are used in a variety of decorative techniques. Here, iron oxide is being spattered through a simple newspaper stencil to create a particular pattern.

4 In throwing, templates can be used to ensure similar repetitive shapes. In this case, they should be made from a durable material such as hardboard. Here a cylinder has been thrown as the basis of the final shape.

5 With the template held firmly at the cylinder's wall, the shape is swelled from the inside until it fills the profile shape.

6 When templates are used in this manner the surface of the thrown pot will reflect mechanical rather than hand-crafted qualities.

THROWING

Hand-forming a mass of soft plastic clay on a rotating wheelhead is called throwing, and the technique can be traced back beyond 2000 BC. Although both the technique and potters' wheels have been refined over the years, the essential methods remain unaltered.

No other forming technique tests clay as much as throwing, and particular care should be taken when preparing clay (see KNEADING and WEDGING). It must be soft, pliable, and sensitive enough to be shaped quickly but firm enough to retain its shape when wet.

The key to successful throwing is the initial process of getting the clay into the center of the wheelhead before shaping commences, called CENTERING. Once this has been successfully completed, a whole range of objects and shapes can be thrown, mostly stemming from simple basic shapes such as plate, bowl, or cylinder forms.

Shallow Open Forms

These are perhaps the easiest to throw since their low profile makes them very stable, and the centrifugal force of the rotating wheelhead virtually wills the clay to spread outwards. The clay mass should be spread over the wheelhead by applying downward pressure with the palm of the hand. It can then be opened by using both thumbs moving in opposite directions, thus creating the inside base and leaving a generous thickness which can be removed during TURNING. The base of any thrown form defines its width: opening too far beyond the base will leave the weight of the wall unsupported and liable to collapse.

Wide forms are difficult to remove from the wheelhead immediately after throwing, so if possible a removable throwing bat should be used, where the form can remain until it has stiffened slightly.

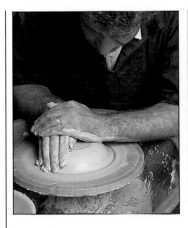

Throwing a shallow open form
1 The base of any thrown form defines its maximum diameter. Apply downward pressure with the palms of both hands to spread the centered clay mass over a larger area of the wheelhead.

The plate is a refinement of the basic process for making a shallow open form. This thrown plate by Seth Cardew employs sure brushstrokes sparingly to produce a deceptively simple surface design.

2 Open out the clay by using both thumbs, pushing them outward in opposite directions to form the inside base. Rest your arms on the wheel tray for stability.

3 Once the shallow dish is opened out as far as the base will allow, the wall is thinned to give the form added height. This is done by taking a firm grip on the clay between thumb and first finger and moving steadily upward, using the other hand as a means of support.

Throwing a cylinder
1 Form the inside base by moving the tip of your thumb from the center of the clay mass outwards. Use your other hand as a support while throwing.

3 Once the cylinder has become too tall to grip between thumb and middle finger, use the middle finger of the non-working hand inside the cylinder while supporting the outside with the working hand. Take a steady hold at the bottom of the cylinder wall and, maintaining steady pressure, raise the hand upward.

5 The raising action should be precisely vertical. There is a natural tendency to lean backward slightly, but try to resist this, as it will cause the cylinder to flare outwards. The raising action is continued until the clay wall has taken up all excess.

7 Any unevenness around rims can be removed with a needle. With the wheelhead rotating slowly, steady the inside rim with the left index finger, and push the needle steadily into the clay wall approximately ¼in. (5mm.) below the lowest point of the rim until it meets your left index finger on the inside. Lift the cut section clear of the rim.

2 In order to add height once the inside base has been formed, grip the clay wall between thumb and middle finger and raise the hand upwards in a steady, gradual motion. The thickened section of clay immediately above the thumb tip will be absorbed as height increases.

4 The section shows the alignment of fingertip inside and knuckle during the lift. Notice the extra thickness of clay which will allow further height. The elbows are tucked into the side for maximum stability and the thumb forms a bridge between the two hands.

6 This section shows how the clay has been economically used to add maximum height to the cylinder. The width of the base is slightly greater than that of the rim, which helps to give stability to the shape.

8 The rim can be smoothed and compressed by applying downward pressure with the index finger while the rim is supported inside and out between thumb and other index finger.

9 Any water which has collected inside the cylinder should be removed with a sponge attached to a stick while the wheelhead rotates.

10 Excess clay from around the outer base edge can be trimmed off with a turning tool. The cylinder is then removed from the wheel by cutting it off with a tautly held wire. The hands must be dry to give a good grip on the wet surface of the cylinder when lifting it off.

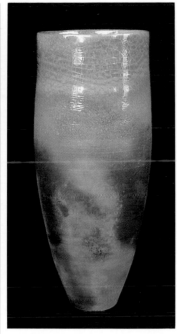

The shape of this tall vase by Gerry Unsworth is a simple development of a basic cylindrically thrown form. Smoking the pot after the glaze firing emphasized the crackle lines in the glaze surface.

Throwing a pouring lip

1 Items such as jugs need some form of spout or pouring lip. On thrown pots, these can be formed while throwing. Ensure that the rim is thick enough to allow for the lip, and start by teasing a section of rim and the area immediately below it upward.

2 When the teased area grows higher than the rim, smooth it by running your thumb and index finger back and forth along it.

3 Finally, use the finger tips to make a clear channel, supporting the lip from below.

Bowl Forms

For these the shape must be swelled and the height of the wall raised in one simultaneous action. Initial shaping of the inside of the bowl is done with the thumb and middle fingers of one hand, while the other hand steadies the emerging outer shape. Particular attention should be paid to the inside curve of the bowl as this determines both its outer shape and the final base and foot thickness.

Care must be taken when removing the bowl from the wheelhead as any sudden movement will distort the rim. If a removable bat is not available, potters often lay a sheet of thin paper across the rim, which acts as an air pocket and helps to prevent distortion. Alternately a hairdryer can be used to stiffen the bowl slightly before removing it.

Cylinders

These can form the basis for many other thrown shapes. Once the base is formed, the wall is raised with pressure from the thumb and middle finger until it has become too tall for fingertips to reach the inside base. At this point the knuckle of one hand is used on the outside with the middle finger of the other hand assisting on the inside. If too much or uneven pressure is exerted, the cylinder wall may tear or weaken. Other common faults such as the wall twisting may occur if the clay is insufficiently lubricated or if the clay was not initially centered properly.

Swelling

This is the shaping technique which enables shapes to grow or expand outwards. The centrifugal force of the wheelhead encourages any pot to flare outwards, and consequently the thrower is often actively working to prevent this from happening. However, where a shape is required to swell in a particular manner, the process takes place mainly while the wall is being raised, with further refinements made afterwards. If an open shape is developed from a cylinder, the walls should be kept thick, as much of the thickness will be used up as the clay expands. If considerable swelling is required, the amount of water should be kept to the minimum, as too much can soften the clay to the extent where it can no longer support itself. Another potential cause of collapse is opening the shape too far beyond the width of the base.

Although initial swelling during the raising process can be done quite quickly, with the wheel rotating at a fast speed, further swelling should progress slowly as even the slightest fault is compounded and exaggerated by a fast-turning wheel. An enclosed shape can be gently inflated to create a fuller, rounder one.

Swelling is used in conjunction with the technique of narrowing or restricting forms, usually referred to as COLLARING. See also STACK THROWING/REPETITION, LIDS AND FITTINGS.

Throwing a bowl
1 A bowl shape grows upward and outward simultaneously. The hand positioning is similar to that used for a cylinder, but the lifting is done in a gentle outward rather than vertical movement.

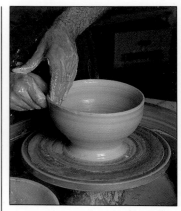

3 A considerable thickness – more than might be expected – should be left around the rim and immediately below it, as this will be used up as the bowl swells outward.

2 Shaping should take place gradually, with successive lifts increasing both diameter and height. Where the base becomes the wall, this should be rounded rather than angular.

4 Any excess clay around the outside base area which can be removed at this stage without detriment to stability should be pared off by turning.

5 This section shows the inside curvature of the bowl, with the wall thrown to the minimum thinness the clay will permit. There is an indication of what clay might have been turned away from the foot at the leather-hard stage and the resulting foot sectioned shape.

This luxuriously decorated lusterware bowl by Sutton Taylor swells confidently outward and upward from its small foot, with the elegant inner curve producing an uninterrupted flow.

This thrown and carved bowl by Peter Lane employs a heavily specked surface achieved through spattering copper oxide onto the surface of the glaze. The carved wing designs which fan outward from the center of the bowl serve to emphasise the bowl's expanding shape.

TURNING

This is the process of trimming off excess clay from around the outside base edge and underneath of a thrown form (these trimmings can be reused – see below). The outside base edge can be turned to some extent immediately after throwing while the clay is still very soft, but the base of a pot is turned when leather-hard.

Aesthetic considerations – the shape and correct feel of the pot – are main reasons for turning, but another factor is the improvement in balance given by a foot rim. The process is a means of adding a final correction to a form rather than one of radical alteration to shape, since at the leather-hard stage the clay will have lost its fluid response to pressure that it had during the throwing stage.

Pieces such as flat dishes and spherical shapes and bowls require extra clay to be left around the base area for stability until they stiffen, but other forms should require only the minimum of turning if they have been thrown correctly. Many experienced production throwers do not need to turn the bases of their wares at all – to do so would merely increase the amount of working time and hence the production costs.

Turning is carried out on the wheel with the pot placed base uppermost in the center. Pots that cannot be balanced in an inverted position should be first secured in a "chuck," which can be thrown to fit and left to stiffen for use. If wrapped in polyethylene after use, chucks can be kept in a usable state for considerable periods of time. Alternately

they can be adapted from existing bisque-fired pots or even plastic flower pots as long as the rim edges are first cushioned with a coil of soft clay to protect the pot placed inside or on top. Items such as jugs with the spout above the rim level will need a pad of clay to cushion the rim and to raise its level above that of the spout.

A variety of differently shaped cutting edges are available from suppliers, but many potters accumulate a variety of home-made and improvised turning tools. There is no right or wrong tool; the only real criterion is that it should cut the clay cleanly and be comfortable to use.

Begin turning by leveling off the base, moving from the center to the edge, which will remove any unevenness. Trim off any ragged edges and define the exact area that the foot rim will occupy before the outside base area of the pot is turned to the required profile. The shape of the foot rim will alter the whole appearance of a pot and must be carefully considered before turning commences. Its shape or size will depend upon the type of form thrown: a small narrow foot may be appropriate for a small bowl, while a large pot will demand a broader base for stability. Foot rims that are comfortable to grip will also be useful when it comes to GLAZING as they enable the pot to be held while dipping into glaze.

Turning should be carried out gradually with only very thin layers pared off. Cutting away clay too fast usually results in the turning tool embedding in the clay wall and either knocking the pot off

center or completely dislodging it. "Chattering" sometimes occurs during turning, recognizable by the development of ripples on the clay surface. It is usually due to the clay being in the wrong condition or the turning tool being insufficiently sharp or insecurely held. Clays which contain a heavy grog content are likely to develop scratch lines along the surface as pieces of grog come to the surface and are dragged along by the turning tool. Such marks can be removed or at least subdued by using a smoothing tool or throwing rib pressed firmly onto the rotating clay surface.

Reclaiming Clay

At any stage before bisque firing (see FIRING), clay can be reprocessed and prepared for reuse. All turned trimmings and unusable dry pieces of clay can be reclaimed, but care must be taken not to include fragments of bisque-fired pottery or to mix clays of different types.

All such pieces should be broken into small pieces and collected in a suitable watertight container, such as a large bucket or garbage can, and covered with water. After leaving for a day or so all the clay will have "slaked" down into a slurry. Excess water lying on the surface is then removed and the slurry spread out onto drying boards or plaster slabs. These can be covered with fabric to prevent any possibility of plaster contamination, also making it easier to turn the clay to assist drying. Once the clay has reached the stage where it is manageable and not too sticky, it can be prepared for use by KNEADING and WEDGING.

2 The pot must be re-centered in an inverted position on the wheelhead before turning can begin. It can then be carefully fixed to the wheelhead with small pieces of clay around the rim.

1 Some turning can be done before the freshly thrown pot is removed from the wheel. How much is possible at this stage will to a large extent be determined by the shape and stability of the pot itself. It is worth remembering that it is a lot quicker to remove clay at this stage than when leather-hard.

3 Taking up a comfortable position, join the fingers of both hands to form a steady link between hands, turning tool and pot. Begin by cutting away any unevenness from the base area and around the outer edge. If the outer edge is particularly ragged, it may be an advantage to use a needle.

5 Begin from the center of the base and work outward, removing only a thin layer of clay each time. Keep the base thickness in mind as you work, to ensure you do not accidentally cut right through it.

Using a "chuck"
1 Thrown pots with narrow or enclosed necks must be inverted into collars or "chucks" to hold them while turning is done. Large bowls can be inverted over chucks if they are too wide to fit a standard wheelhead.

3 Where a pot has an uneven section of rim, such as a pouring lip, a collar of clay can be formed on the wheelhead to accommodate the inverted pot. Here, a small section has been cut out of the collar so that the pouring lip of the jug can sit in it without fear of damage.

4 Once the base and outer edge are level, the lines defining the proposed foot rim can be marked in with the edge of the tool to identify the edges you will be working to.

6 The outer edge of the foot rim can then be defined. The clay will normally be at its thickest at this point, and it is often surprising how much clay can be removed. It is important to keep checking the shape of the foot as it develops, as it must appear to grow naturally from the main body of the pot.

2 Chucks can be thrown especially for particular pots and then kept wrapped tightly in soft polyethylene until the next time they are required. Once positioned in the chuck, turning can be done in the way described. If the pot is in the right state for turning, the clay will pare off easily in long strips.

Reclaiming clay
Dry scraps of old unused clay, trimmings, and throwing mishaps can all be used again. A plastic container is needed to collect all the scraps. Water is poured in to cover them, and once it has all slaked down into a slurry, it can be spread over a slab until dry enough to prepare for re-use.

WEDGING

This is one of the two processes, the other being KNEADING, which potters employ to ensure their clay is in a workable condition before use. It helps to thoroughly mix the clay and expel any pockets of air.

Small amounts of clay can be hand wedged, which simply involves tearing the clay into two, smacking the two lumps together sharply, and repeating the process until well mixed. Large pieces can be wedged on a work bench or other suitable surface such as a concrete slab. This should be absorbent to ensure that the clay does not stick to it. Cut the clay mass into two using a wire. Slam one section down onto the other, then give the mass a quarter turn, cut into two, and repeat the process until the clay is of an even consistency and free of any air pockets.

Clay should be wedged when it has passed the sticky stage but is still soft; the wedging surface will absorb some of the water. The process can also be used to soften clay which has become slightly stiffer than required. In this case, slice it into layers, indent each surface, coat it with a thick layer of slurry, and press the layers together. The stiffer clay will take up the slurry as wedging proceeds, and the whole mass will become soft. If cracks and splits appear at the outset, however, the clay is too dry and is best left to soak for a time.

Wedging small pieces of clay
1 Small pieces of clay can be hand wedged very simply by tearing the clay into two parts and then smacking them together sharply.

2 This simple process should be repeated until the clay is well mixed. It should be borne in mind, however, that any clay held for long periods does tend to dry out.

2 Lift up one half and slam it down onto the other one from a comfortable height. The larger the amount of clay, the less force is required.

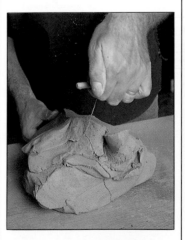

Wedging large pieces of clay
1 Large pieces of clay should be wedged on the surface of a sturdy bench or slab positioned at waist height. It is important that the surface is porous so that the clay does not stick. Begin by cutting the clay block in half with a wire.

3 The process of repeatedly cutting and slamming the block of clay serves to mix it and remove any air.

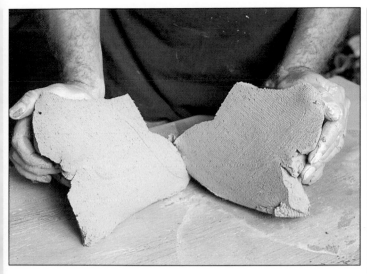

4 Looking at a sliced section of the wedged clay will quickly reveal whether it has been sufficiently mixed and is air-free. Wedging is a preparation process normally used in conjunction with that of kneading.

Softening stiff clay
1 Slightly stiff clay can be softened up by wedging in softer clay. Slice up the clay slab and indent the surface.

3 When the separate layers have been formed into a multiple sandwich, cut the resulting slab into two or more sections.

2 Cover the indented surfaces with softer clay of the same type.

4 A period of wedging will then mix the softer and stiffer clays together. If there are large amounts of clay, however, it may be more practical to slake all the clay down before preparing it for use.

PART TWO

THEMES

Although some people still approach pottery-making with preconceived ideas about what constitutes a piece of pottery or will acceptably pass as one, such constraints are rapidly disappearing. Over recent years, the horizons have widened, and few ideas or themes are now deemed unsuitable to explore in clay. This new freedom has resulted in a rich and varied range of work that often has no more than the most tenuous links with traditional pottery other than the techniques used to produce it.

The reader of this book will quickly realize that I have deliberately avoided making personal judgements. I have not raised such questions as whether a work falls into the category of sculpture rather than pottery; whether a piece should be called a work of "art" or one of "craft;" or whether domestic ware has greater or lesser value than an individual and completely non-functional object.

These matters, which have given rise to intense debate over the past decade, are outside the scope of this book. My purpose here is to identify and explain a variety of pottery techniques – some simple and traditional, some unusual and more complex –

and suggest approaches which you may find stimulating and exciting. I hope that using the book for reading and reference will enable you to produce work which, even if not initially technically brilliant, will lay the foundation for a continued exploration of the rich world of pottery and ceramics, thus increasing both competence and personal satisfaction.

Technique should never be seen as an end in itself, but total involvement in the way of making things can provide its own kind of inspiration. Technical exploration may encourage some potters to stretch themselves and their materials to their utmost limits, thus extending and re-defining previously accepted boundaries. Others may find themselves involved in an all-consuming struggle with materials in the quest to extend and adapt techniques and materials to meet their specific requirements and express their personal preoccupations.

The purpose of this second section of the book is to look at finished examples of the work of a variety of potters who have utilized the techniques described and illustrated in the first, alphabetical section. In sifting through the vast number of examples, certain themes or groupings have naturally suggested themselves as offering natural comparisons, not of good versus bad technique, but of different approaches. Sometimes the basic shapes or methods are similar, but the ideas and final results widely divergent, while in other cases there is a similarity in theme but a completely different use of materials and technique. The range of interpretations within any one area is vast; a thrown bowl, for instance, although a simple shape involving one of the most basic forming processes, can be almost endlessly varied. The themes have been chosen as ideas which could spark off new approaches, but because working methods can never be divorced from the design process, I have also laid some emphasis on the particular characteristics of each of the main forming techniques. We all have it in us to respond creatively to particular stimuli, and I hope that by introducing you to the work of a wide and varied range of potters – some familiar and others less so – you will be inspired to develop your own ideas with a sound knowledge of how to do so.

NATURAL AND ORGANIC FORMS

Potter Michael Bayley says that his ideas "stem from landscape, seascape, cloudscape, skyscape, trees, rocks, and sometimes include man-made shapes." David Jones, in a statement supporting his RAKU pieces, lists the range of objects that he collects and from which he draws inspiration. "Shells, polished by the sea; shells, encrusted with barnacles. Stones tumbled by a river; stones cracked and broken, revealing their million-year-old histories. Old cans found beyond the high-water line rusted to distortion. The exact patterns produced by the vegetative world in the midst of apparent chaos. In my raku work I endeavor to synthesize these contrary forces...."

Our natural environment provides a constant source of inspiration. The patterns, shapes, colors, and textures we see around us all form the basis for ceramic exploration, while a simple shell, piece of driftwood, or the section of a plant or flower can serve to supply the initial stimulus from which an idea can develop. The starting point for any piece of work is likely to be a variety of influences which overlap and interact to produce a personal response on the part of the potter, and because each person is a separate individual, no two potters will produce the same work even if their initial inspiration is similar.

These differences in approach can be seen clearly in the work of Mary Rogers (page 98) and Elsa Rady (opposite). In these pieces both potters are concerned with an exploration of the qualities of plants and flowers, and both use porcelain as the ceramic medium, but their pieces convey virtually opposite qualities. Mary Rogers has responded to the fragile, vulnerable delicacy of an opening flower with its undulating folds and markings, and has reproduced the folded qualities in her work by forming the thin sheet of soft porcelain in a small, deep bowl mold. Elsa Rady's "Lily" expresses the sharp-edged rigidity which is also a fundamental characteristic of many plants and flowers. The thin, crisp-edged porcelain shape has been thrown and then cut (see FACETING).

While some potters' work relates very closely to its source of origin, others will extend and develop an idea to the extent where the final work takes on a totally new identity, bearing no more than a vague or emotive reference to the original source. In neither case does the potter set out to produce a clay replica of the stimulus, but rather a synthesis or a response which may heighten an aspect which has particular personal relevance. The work of Michael Bayley, for example, is concerned with elements of the landscape, and his carefully selected clay mixtures produce color combinations which themselves reflect these interests. The addition of sands and grog (see ADDITIVES) and his range of colored clay mixes provide him with coarse, open, subtle-toned clays varying from light cream to strong dark browns.

Peter Lane's work also reflects a preoccupation with the landscape, and many of his bowl forms provide a basis for exploring the visual potential of various aspects of it, such as the patterns created by light and shade. Shapes selected and simplified from his observations and sketches are translated into surface qualities such as color and texture by his use of glazes, or form the starting point for the pierced and carved decoration which is a feature of his work (see PIERCED DECORATION).

The forms of Karen Chesney rely on a detailed knowledge of birds. Her inventive method of constructing shapes from thrown sections combines technical skill and careful observation, so that her shapes, although perfectly convincing, are decorative rather than literal.

Christine Constant produces RAKU pieces which are both technically and visually intriguing. Her work includes objects which have an obvious relationship with marine forms but at the same time have a mechanical quality which could suggest gear mechanisms or old-fashioned tools of an era long past.

ELSA RADY
Lily
The title of this thrown and cut porcelain form confirms its obvious links with natural flower forms. The work's simplicity of form, emphasized by the simple white glaze, almost disguises the technical achievement involved in throwing it.

◀ MARY ROGERS
Porcelain form

The fragile qualities of an opening flower are beautifully captured in this handbuilt porcelain piece. The translucency of the porcelain and the oxide decoration (see COLORING) over the white-glazed surface combine to produce an effective impression of the mottled markings often seen on natural objects. The piece was made from a thin sheet of porcelain which was carefully eased into a mold, the folded quality being a direct result of the forming process. The small foot was added from a thin strip of clay once the shape had stiffened sufficiently to work on further.

▲ MICHAEL BAYLEY
Landscape plaque

The striped patterns in Bayley's work were produced by thinly slicing a block of laminated clays of contrasting color (see AGATEWARE). The thin sections were then inlaid into the plaque by rolling them into the pliable clay surface, and paper-thin areas of different-colored clays were inlaid in the same manner. This process gives him considerable scope for compositional decisions when designing each piece of work. His unglazed surfaces show the open character and natural coloring of his blended clays. These, containing colored sands and grog (see ADDITIVES), echo the qualities of the natural landscape, which is his inspiration.

▶ MICHAEL BAYLEY
Slabbed stoneware pot

The agate strips of applied decoration on this dark-surfaced slab pot were sliced off from a prepared block of colored clays (see AGATEWARE) and applied to the surface using slurry. The tree-like surface pattern shows a skilful use of a range of neutral earth colors. These were made by combining Potclay's St. Thomas Body with a chocolate one to achieve a mid-tone, and then adding a red and white-bodied clay to extend the range (see COLORING). This unglazed piece was once-fired (see GLAZING) to 2300°F (1260°C).

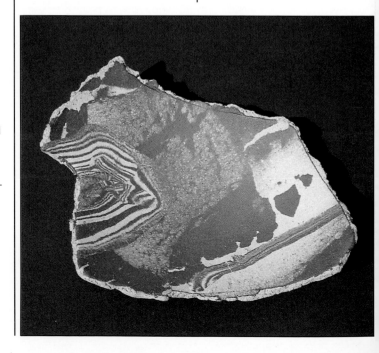

JO CONNELL
Vase with floral pattern

The decoration here evolved from an interest in Art Deco motifs. Thin floral patterns, made from a variety of colored clays, were inlaid into a slab of white stoneware clay, which was then pressed into an elliptical two-piece mold (see PRESS MOLDING). The joints have been emphasized through the shape rather than any attempt being made to disguise them. Once the slabs began to stiffen and shrink away from the plaster surface, the two sections of the mold were married together, and a coil was applied to form the rim. The piece was bisque fired to 1832°F (1000°C). It was glazed on the inside simply to make it watertight, and was glaze fired to 2273°F (1245°C) in an electric kiln (see FIRING and GLAZING).

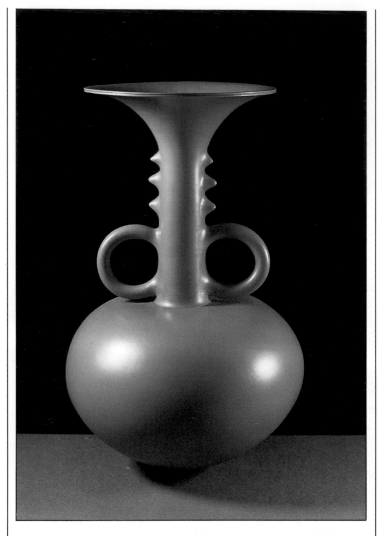

◄ MAGDALENE ODUNDO
Handbuilt burnished form
This rounded, full-bellied, coiled form employs a decorative notched neck. The carefully considered ring handles serve to add a hint of functionalism to the otherwise austere, highly polished shape.

▼ MAGDALENE ODUNDO
Handbuilt burnished form
The natural simplicity of this form evokes the surface qualities and symmetry of gourds and other exotic fruit and vegetables. The earthy clay coloring, oval rim, and angled neck further emphasize the natural qualities.

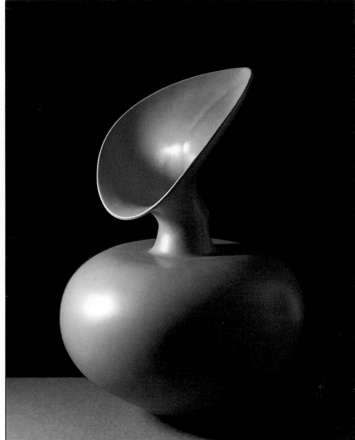

MAGD A LENE ODUNDO
Handbuilt burnished and smoked form
A mastery of technique and proportional balance is displayed in this elegant vase. The rich, highly polished surface shows the subtle variations of color that can be achieved by the SMOKING method.

BARBARA MANUEL
Textured form

The heavily textured surface, reminiscent of weathered rock, is a very important element of this pot. It was achieved by Manuel's particular method of construction, which involves pressing small pieces of clay together, with the thumb impressions deliberately left unsmoothed. After bisque firing, colored slips and glazes were brushed on to the surface (see GLAZING), and the pot was oxidized-fired (see FIRING) at a temperature of 2264°F (1240°C).

◀ KAREN CHESNEY
Bird forms

Chesney's charming, highly
decorative pieces are thrown in
sections using a white stoneware
or porcelain body. Once leather-
hard, the sections are assembled
and decorated with a variety of
colored slips (see SLIP
DECORATION), employing RESIST
and SGRAFFITO techniques. All her
pieces are bisque fired to 1832°F
(1000°C) and then glazed with a
transparent glaze, which is then
fired to a temperature of 2300°F
(1260°C). Finally, lusters are
applied in order to bring out
further detail, and the work is fired
once again to a temperature of
1382°F (750°C), just sufficient to
soften the glaze surface so that
the lusters become permanently
fixed (see FIRING and GLAZING).

▲ PETER LANE
Hedgerow bowl

The decoration of this thrown
porcelain bowl was achieved by
carving and PIERCING the wall. As
the name of the piece implies,
Lane's starting point was careful
observation of the effects made
by branches intertwining and
linking together in hedges. A
white matt glaze was applied and
the piece was fired (see FIRING) in
an electric kiln at 2300°F
(1260°C).

DAVID JONES
Raku pot

Jones draws inspiration for his shapes and surfaces from a variety of sources, including both natural objects like shells and pebbles, and discarded man-made ones which show the effects of weathering and nature, such as rusted and distorted cans. The metallic lustered surfaces have been achieved by incorporating various metal oxides into the RAKU glaze and then reduction FIRING.

▲ G. WEIGEL
Sculptural pot

In this piece, qualities of rock and boulder forms are evoked through the simple angular shape and handbuilt construction. The implied split down the center dominates the composition as the immediate focal point. The earthy surface coloring enhances the quiet naturalness without losing any of the surface detail.

▶ IVES MOTTY
Scuptural form

Here roundness is contrasted with sharp angular planes to emphasize the qualities often found in rocks and stones. The use of pale, neutral gray coloring enhances the organic associations.

◀ CHRISTINE CONSTANT
Blue dial with pierced horn and golden dial with jeweled horn

Of the many influences which can be traced through Constant's work, the most central and recurrent one is marine forms. A variety of techniques was used for these pieces, including a sophisticated form of APPLIED DECORATION, soft clay "facing." The combined techniques of SLIP CASTING, PRESS MOLDING, and handbuilding all feature in her work as appropriate.

▲ CHRISTINE CONSTANT
Blue/copper striped spiral vessel

Many of this potter's RAKU fired vessels contain well-defined spiral elements which clearly evoke shell structures. In this piece, they are given further emphasis by the effective use of surface lines radiating outward from point to rim. The powerful blue and copper-bronze colorings are features associated with the glaze effects obtainable by the raku process.

CHRISTINE CONSTANT
Spiked and striped spiral vessels

One of Constant's recurring preoccupations is with old tools, machinery parts, and other defunct man-made objects. The spiral qualities seen here may owe as much to these as to her fascination with marine forms, while the fierce, spiky, angular qualities conjure rather more brutal images. There is an interesting use of the resist technique (see RESIST DECORATION) in both pieces where she has left some areas as strong, unglazed lines. These have become blackened after reduction following the RAKU firing.

CHRISTINE CONSTANT
Dial and gold horn
The use of sophisticated PRESS MOLDING and SLIP CASTING techniques ensures a highly individual development of ideas in Constant's work. Some of her imaginary marine forms look almost like living creatures, blending with their natural environment of sea or sand. The exploration of related forms is another important theme in her work.

CHRISTINE CONSTANT
Dial with triangled horn
The severe, angled nature of the spiky dial section is continued through even the more rounded forms of the horn, with the triangular scale-like surface evoking the qualities of chain mail. This piece conveys something of the "organized" patterns often found in nature – and even the geometrically patterned "nose" could well be one of the regular and clearly defined patterns seen on the wings of an insect or sea creature.

FUNCTIONAL AND DOMESTIC POTTERY

The human race has always needed containers and vessels for a range of different purposes, and it is thought that the earliest clay vessels were copied from those made from natural materials such as curved sections of tree bark, hollowed-out gourds, or stretched animal skins. It is probable, although not provable, that the first pieces of pottery were produced accidentally, the result of lining baskets with clay to make them watertight. Even after pottery had become an established method of producing durable utilitarian ware, there was a tendency to copy the styles of other objects, particularly metal ones.

Clay quickly became the most widely used material for storage vessels, and the role of the potter became a central one in society. Just as the volume of pottery production increased, so too did the development of pottery for specific uses. Jars and deep bowls which may have originally been made to store grain or other food, with wide open necks to facilitate emptying and filling, developed into taller and thinner shapes better suited to storing liquids, such as water, wine, beer, or oils and ointments.

The earliest pots were handbuilt, by a method similar to the COILING technique used today, and even before the use of the wheel became widespread (approximately 2000 B.C.), pots were most often rounded. The introduction of the wheel, although originally no more than a rough disc on a movable base, had a profound effect on pottery. Shapes became more refined, with thinner walls, while the much faster process of THROWING enabled increased production. Similar advances were taking place in FIRING and kiln technology, and the development of glazed rather than simply burnished surfaces (see BURNISHING) resulted in a parallel increase in both durability and function.

In some ways little has changed over the past few thousand years; although fashions and trends come and go, the most commonly produced form of pottery today is still functional domestic ware. Industrial and semi-industrial processes have, of course, influenced potters over recent years, but even so, with a few notable exceptions, the vast majority of individual potters still rely on the wheel as a means of producing cost-effective quality items.

To a greater or lesser extent, historical and cultural influences can be seen clearly running through the work of most potters. Particular processes or techniques from a period in history are often explored by contemporary potters, while others take a whole philosophy of working from another culture. For example, it is difficult to discuss domestic ware without reference to Oriental pottery, and thus the work of such pioneer potters as Bernard Leach and his contemporaries, who were deeply influenced by the East. Many of today's techniques can be traced back to the specific periods during which they became established. German salt-glazed pottery, majolica decoration, and Staffordshire slipwares, to name but a few, have all been influential, and many modern potters have used their qualities as starting points for personal exploration (see MAJOLICA and SLIP DECORATION).

The range of functional pottery items is more or less unlimited. Just as early civilizations adapted old shapes to new ones to fulfil different functions, so modern potters slowly evolve new ideas from existing ones to meet newly created needs. For instance, the simple rounded soup bowl has evolved to become a shallow flat-based bowl suited to serving pasta. "Oven proof" ware has been made for a very long time, but nowdays many functional pieces must also be "suitable for use in a freezer, microwave, and dishwasher."

As function and purpose have slowly changed, traditional items, while maintaining their original purpose, have undergone a process of gradual refinement and evolution. The teapots of Walter Keeler and the Hungarian potter Sandor Dobany are designed to fulfil the same function as any other teapot, yet are a long way removed from what we might consider a traditional shape. Similarly, Jane

Hamlyn's extremely functional and pleasing oval salt-glazed casserole is very different to the classic casserole shapes of Svend Bayer, although in their own way both are extremely successful.

SVEND BAYER
Stoneware casseroles

Although essentially functional in nature, these emphasize the individual character of every wheel-thrown piece of pottery. The markings on the surface are typical of a wood firing where clay comes into direct contact with flame.

▲ JENNY CLARKE
Boxes with thrown lids
The blue and green slips used for the decorative motifs on the lids are modified in strength by the white glaze that covers them, but the details of the decorations are still clearly visible. Considerable precision and accuracy are required to produce boxes whose lids fit securely.

► JENNY CLARKE
Lidded jars
These stoneware jars feature dark iron-bearing slips and sgraffito decoration under a white matt glaze. The simple yet effective pattern gives a sense of unity to the pieces, although they vary in both size and function.

◄ JENNY CLARKE
Stoneware cheese dish
The deep green semi
transparent glaze on this thrown
dish partly fills the incised
decoration to produce a subtle
effect. The curved handle echoes
the rounded qualities of both
shape and decoration.

◄ JANE HAMLYN
Salt-glazed oval casserole
This very practical piece of pottery is obviously designed for use, but the potter has not had to compromise anything of her very personal and individual style. Textures rouletted into the soft clay surface combine well with the textured surface of the salt glaze.

► GUS MABELSON
Salt-glazed teapot and stand
Salt-glazed domestic ware, which has increased in popularity over recent years, is often a successful adaptation of traditional techniques to satisfy modern needs. This well-crafted piece employs IMPRESSING and APPLIED DECORATION to good effect.

GERRY UNSWORTH
Smoked ginger jar
A piece need not be plain to be
functional, as this elegant jar
demonstrates. The glazed and
lustered surface was also smoked
in order to achieve the final effect.
The cup lid brings the rounded
curves of the jar to a pleasing
conclusion.

DAPHNE CARNEGY
Domestic group

Tin-glazed MAJOLICA decorative techniques employing oxides and commercial colors have been used to achieve these highly decorative surfaces. The stylized designs incorporate a variety of techniques, including brushing, sponging, and stippling color onto the freshly glazed surface (see GLAZING).

DAPHNE CARNEGY
Large dish

The graphic floral decoration on this decorative but functional dish displays a skilful and creative use of the surface area.

DART POTTERY
Domestic ware

The richly colored designs employed by the Dart Pottery have been developed by potter and designer Janice Tchalenko. The brightly colored surface patterning was a new departure in the decoration of domestic ware.

◄ SABINA TEUTEBERG
Mugs
The simple, practical shapes, produced by the JIGGERING AND JOLLYING processes, are enlivened by brightly colored modern designs which would add sparkle to any kitchen.

◄ SABINA TEUTEBERG
Large plate
Here boldly geometric decoration provides a visual feast which in no way detracts from function. Inlaid coloring (see INLAY) has provided a simple but effective graphic treatment of surface pattern.

SABINA TEUTEBERG
Plate
The range of tans, yellows, and oranges contrasts sharply with the prominent dashes of blue. Such daring combinations and approaches were virtually unheard of in ceramic decoration even a few years ago, but have now become fashionable in ceramics as well as furnishings, fabrics, and other household equipment.

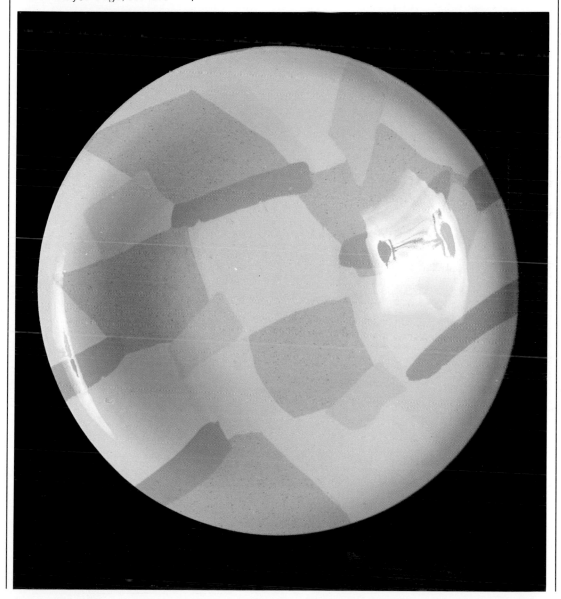

STEVEN HILL
Melon pitcher
This functional piece is a good example of the individuality of style a potter can achieve through a personal approach to even the most basic of forms. It was altered (see ALTERING THROWN SHAPES) immediately after throwing to emphasize a pouring channel, and the richly colored surface was achieved through the application of several glazes. The handle was made by the EXTRUSION technique.

STEVEN HILL
Thrown urn
The immediacy and directness of THROWING are wonderfully conveyed by this piece. The shape was subtly altered (see ALTERING THROWN SHAPES) immediately after throwing, and the incised lines (see INCISING) on the surface impart a certain tension to the shape. The red blush which can be seen among the fluid mix of glaze color is a feature of many copper-bearing glazes fired in a reduction atmosphere. The work of this potter is normally once-fired only (see FIRING and GLAZING).

WALTER KEELER
Saltware jug
Although primarily conceived and produced as a functional piece of pottery, the modern design suggests sculptural rather than functional qualities. The extruded handle (see EXTRUSION), which effectively bridges the base ridges and rim, adds further interest to the form.

▲ WALTER KEELER
Salt-glazed teapot

This exuberant thrown form is a good example of how the separate – and sometimes disparate – elements of function, decoration, and sculpture can be combined.

▶ WALTER KEELER
Lidded saltware jar

This impressive jar suggests metallic qualities reminiscent of containers made from sheet metal, while still retaining the essential qualities and characteristics of clay. Like most of Keeler's work, this was thrown in sections, altered (see ALTERING THROWN SHAPES), and then assembled.

▲ DAVID SCOTT
Teapot
Much of Scott's work is concerned with a personal interpretation of traditional forms. The rounded qualities of his teapots, which often combine different forming techniques such as EXTRUSION, THROWING, and handbuilding, convey the sort of qualities normally associated with "soft sculpture."

▲ SABINA TEUTEBERG
Jug
The proportions of the jug have been explored in a very personal way by this potter, whose imaginative use of semi-industrial processes enables a high degree of individualism. The bold patterning was achieved by a carefully considered use of colored inlaid clays (see AGATEWARE and INLAY).

SABINA TEUTEBERG
Large jug
Although this piece was
designed primarily with function
in mind, there is an inherent
sense of fun in the enlarged
spout, shaped like a toucan bill,
and the exaggerated handle.

SURFACE TREATMENT

It is not unusual for potters to become so wrapped up in some specific aspect of technique – whether a decorative one or one associated with the forming process – that it dominates his or her whole approach. It is obvious, however, that the best pieces of pottery are not those in which only one element is exceptional, but those whose different parts or processes combine together to form a harmonious whole.

Particular surface qualities can be obtained in a number of ways. Some are a direct consequence of the type of clay used, or a particular way of treating it. The smooth, highly polished surfaces of Magdalene Odundo's pots show the particular quality given by BURNISHING the leather-hard stage. Mention has already been made of the potential of ADDITIVES introduced to the clay at the appropriate stage of preparation or decoration, and there is a vast array of ingredients (including other clays) that can be used to ensure that clay behaves in a specific manner. Additives can take the form of coloring stains, or they can be ingredients which react with the clay during the firing process. This effect can be seen in the work of Ewen Henderson, who introduces a variety of materials which melt at a lower temperature than the clay, and ooze out of the surface during the firing.

Particular glazes are known for their potential in creating specific surfaces and characteristics, indeed the names given to many of them – "oxblood," "oilspot," and "hare's fur" for example – describe their predominant color or texture.

But although particular glazes have the potential for creating specific effects, it is impossible to isolate the effect of a glaze from the part played by the firing process, as this affects both clay and glaze. For example, the introduction of salt into the firing chamber combines with the clay to produce the recognizable salt-glazed surface, but only if the temperature is sufficiently high. Crystalline glazes will not actually produce crystals unless very specific firing procedures are carried out to encourage the crystals to grow during the firing process, and

oxblood glazes, which are high in copper content, require a reduction atmosphere in which to produce their distinctive reds. Even the most simple or basic glazes will behave differently according to whether they are fired in an oxidizing or reducing atmosphere, while the colors characteristic of a RAKU firing are as much to do with the actual firing process as with the glazes used.

The FIRING process, on the other hand, can sometimes be separated out as the predominant factor in producing a particular surface quality. The effects of the flame coming into direct contact with the clay surface, as it does in a wood-fired kiln, leaves a warm flashing mark on the unprotected surface, and sawdust firing and pit firing also have a direct effect on the clay. Sawdust can be used to achieve a deep black color on unglazed clay, if placed around the pot and confined in a saggar during the firing. The distinctive blackened pots of John Leach are examples of this method.

Surface qualities can still be created even after glaze firing, using a variety of techniques such as the application of on-glaze lusters and enamels, multiple glazes, or even SGRAFFITO. A less common texturing method is to sandblast the surface, which can be done after glaze firing or at any earlier stage after the pot is dry. The process involves directing a high-pressure jet of sand at the surface, which eats into it regardless of whether it is glazed or not.

Patterning can be done by using resists (see RESIST DECORATION) such as specially prepared latex mixes, or simply tape, and the same technique can be used as a means of producing texture. This can be seen in the work of Harvey Sadow, who achieves remarkable surfaces by a combination of sandblasting, multiple firing, and the applications of different-colored slips.

HARVEY SADOW
Pot
The richly colored and textured surface was achieved by a combination of techniques: the application of colored slips, sandblasting the surface, and multiple RAKU firings.

◀ MARIAN GAUNCE
Laminated porcelain bowl
Here the method of structure is
also the decoration. The precisely
patterned surface is the result of
the painstaking joining together
of small, intricate sections. Each
piece is dried out with extreme
care over a period of several
weeks to minimize the risk of
cracking when the joined
sections dry out.

▼ MARIAN GAUNCE
Laminated porcelain tray
A combination of black and white
stained porcelain has been used
to achieve an effective
monochromatic piece with a very
graphic use of geometric
patterning.

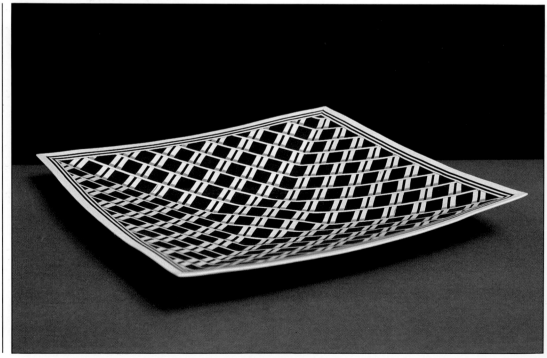

MARIAN GAUNCE
Laminated deep bowl
This piece was made by a type of
PRESS MOLDING technique
involving molds of three or more
pieces. Three or more sections
are made, laid into the mold in
turn, and carefully joined
together. The rim, which serves to
unify the piece, was added
separately.

PETER LANE
Porcelain bowl with carved rim and white crackle glaze
The pronounced crackle in the glaze is an important feature of this bowl, considerably enhancing the porcelain's translucent, fragile beauty.

▼ JOHN LEACH
Saggar-fired deep bowl
The robust yet simple shape of this thrown bowl is enhanced by the whitened line that flashes around the outer surface. It was fired in a saggar partly filled with sawdust in a wood-fired stoneware kiln (see FIRING).

JOHN LEACH
Saggar-fired thrown urn
This functional form is simple, direct, and ageless. The effect of the saggar FIRING is seen in the strong contrasts between the richly blackened surface and the whitened band which circles the form, providing a visual statement of the involvement of fire in the potting process.

FELICITY AYLIEFF
Agate inlaid vase
This potter's handbuilt forms are distinctive for their highly decorative surface treatment, achieved by a technique related to AGATEWARE. She joins coils of different colored clays which, when twisted or rolled, produce an infinite variety of pattern. Thinly cut layers from these sections are then inlaid into the surface of the forms. The stark black base color of this piece creates a powerful contrast to the intricately patterned areas.

▲ ARCHIE McCALL
Stoneware dish

The potter has used multiple glaze applications, resist areas (see RESIST DECORATION) reworked with lively, flowing brushwork, and gold lusters, all of which combine to produce an extremely rich and decorative surface.

◀ FELICITY AYLIEFF
Agate inlaid bowl

The simple motifs interrupt and contrast with the almost marbled effect of the surface decoration. This was cut from AGATEWARE sections and once dry, the inlaid areas were carefully rubbed down to reveal the full effect of the pattern. After vitrifying – at 2228°F (1220°C) – the unglazed surface was polished to produce a smooth, stone-like finish.

ELSIE BLUMER
Porcelain bottle with blue crystals
Encouraging the formation of large, clearly defined crystals within a glaze requires some experience and willingness to experiment. The glaze must contain specific ingredients, and the FIRING cycle must also be carefully controlled.

KRISTIANSEN
Sphere
This form has proved an extremely effective vehicle for the calligraphic style of decoration chosen. Close examination of the surface reveals the visual puzzle of other partly concealed letters.

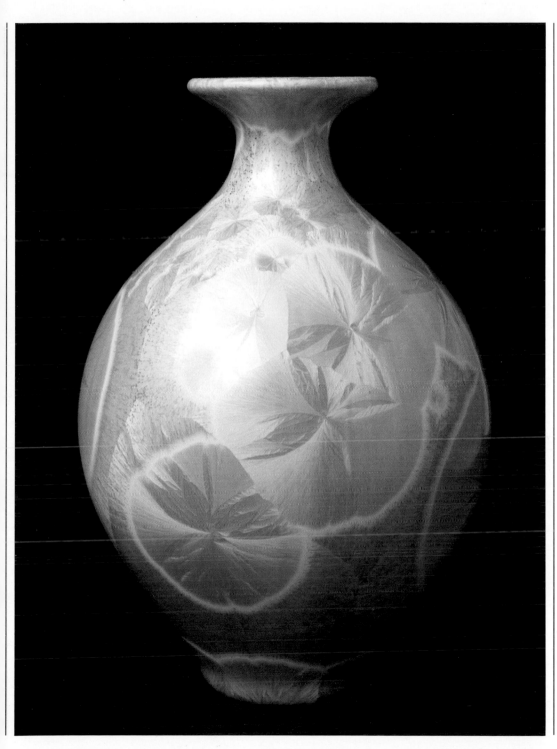

ELSIE BLUMER
Porcelain bottle with large tan crystals
The marvellous large crystals on the surface of this thrown porcelain bottle are a considerable technical feat. They were formed while the glaze was in a very fluid state, and in order to prevent the base from sticking to the kiln shelf, the bottle was fired on a special support.

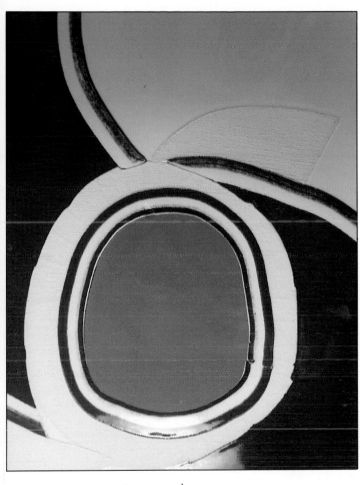

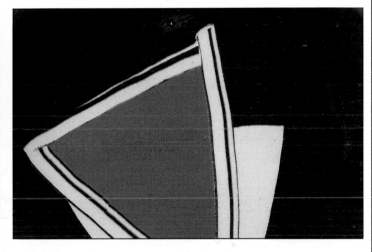

◀ SABINA TEUTEBERG
Dish
The bold geometric design is both simple and effective. The clay was pressed through a bench roller and inlaid with different-colored clays before jollying (see JIGGERING AND JOLLYING). A simple transparent glaze forms a final functional coating for the design.

SABINA TEUTEBERG
Dish (details)
The different colors of the inlaid clays can be clearly seen in these details.

◄ ELIZABETH FRITSCH
Gray vase

The potter has successfully created the illusion of three-dimensional objects appearing to float across the surface of her pot. She has used colored slips, painting the "objects" carefully to reflect the way the forms alter in shape as they move.

▲ JANET LEACH
Thrown and altered pots

The rich surface colors, which include off-white through to orange and black variations, are a direct consequence of the type of FIRING the pieces have undergone. This range is commonly achieved by wood firing, as the pots are often in direct contact with the flames in the kiln.

ELIZABETH FRITSCH
Handbuilt pot
The flat-sided surface has been
painted with a number of pale-
colored slips. The decoration
evolved from the potter's
interpretation of piano keys.

SCULPTURAL AND ABSTRACT FORMS

All art styles and movements, whether the particular discipline is painting, architecture, sculpture, or pottery, are interlinked, sometimes even inseparable, since both the thought process and techniques involve an integration of ideas which cross activity boundaries. Major styles in art can be seen reflected in the pottery styles of the time; for instance, there is a clear and obvious relationship between the painted *maiolica* wares of 15th- and 16th-century Italy and the Renaissance painting style. It is also interesting to note the emergence at this time of the individual ceramic artist, whose work began to command similar prices to those of the artists.

Artists of world importance, such as Paul Gauguin and Pablo Picasso, explored the potential of ceramics as a vehicle for personal expression. The works of these artists and many others, such as Miró, Arp, Chagall, the later Abstract Expressionists, and Pop artists, can all be seen as influential in the development of trends which have influenced the work of many individual potters – and sometimes entire cultures.

In this century, pottery, ceramics, sculptural pottery – call it what you will – has taken account of influences which have been important in other art movements. There are people now working with clay who see themselves in the broad role of sculptor or fine artist, using clay and other ceramic materials and processes to translate their ideas into reality. Often these artists totally lack the traditional concept of "potting" as related to the vessel or any other category of clay object.

Some people still find it difficult to accept that ceramics can – and should – be used just like any other expressive medium. Some of them think that paintings are only "real" art if they refer directly to reality, with the implication that creative and artistic skills require a sort of photographic realism, as if work of an abstract nature "can be done by anyone." Once the notion of function or utility is removed from a piece of pottery, the same questions arise. It is easy to focus on a piece of domestic ware and discuss its merits of craftsmanship and design for use, but when one is confronted with a clay object which cannot be used, and is not necessarily decorative either, it becomes difficult to define whether it is good, bad, or even relevant.

It is interesting to look at the different uses clay has as a surface in two dimensions, as an artist uses a canvas, or as a material for the production of free-standing sculptural forms, or for the production of objects which fall somewhere between these two. Sandy Brown, for example, uses color so freely and expressively that her plate becomes simply a canvas for her art, while in the piece entitled "Picture," the Hungarian potter Gyozo Lorincz takes a sheet or slab of clay and organizes symbols or motifs on it.

Relief panels are an example of ceramics falling between two and three dimensions. The work of the potter Ruth Duckworth has encompassed both large relief panels and three-dimensional sculptural forms. Studio potters frequently explore ceramic forms as sculptural objects in parallel with standard lines of domestic or functional pieces, resulting in a small quantity of personal or individual forms. The normal processes for the production of domestic lines are adapted to fulfil different criteria. If the potter normally works on the wheel, for example, the resulting sculptural forms may still relate closely to the vessel. The thrown and assembled vessels by Hans Coper and the winged form by Colin Pearson illustrate this. Both have unmistakable sculptural affinities while maintaining essentially "thrown" qualities.

◀ PETER COSENTINO
Sections

This piece evolved from considerations of proportion and balance with reference to bottle forms. Although altered and reassembled, it remains essentially a thrown piece. It has pink and white speckled slips under a low-fired transparent glaze, and was sawdust smoked after glaze firing (see SMOKING).

▲ COLIN PEARSON
Winged form

This thrown and altered stoneware form incorporates pure sculptural elements in the applied sections that form the wings. The surface treatment demonstrates the clay's texture, its malleable qualities, and the immediacy of THROWING as a means of both production and shaping.

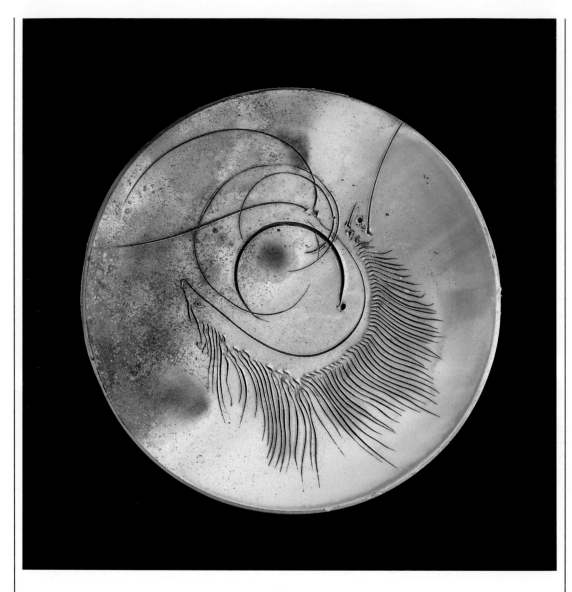

FRANK BOYDEN
Skeleton plate
This wood-fired porcelain plate is
unglazed. It has been decorated
with colored stains and INCISING.

HANS COPER
Thistle form
This composite thrown form is an exploration of proportion and contrasts. The dry light-colored slip of the external surface contrasts sharply with the rich darkness of the interior. The concentric lines on the surface reinforce the particular qualities seen in thrown ware.

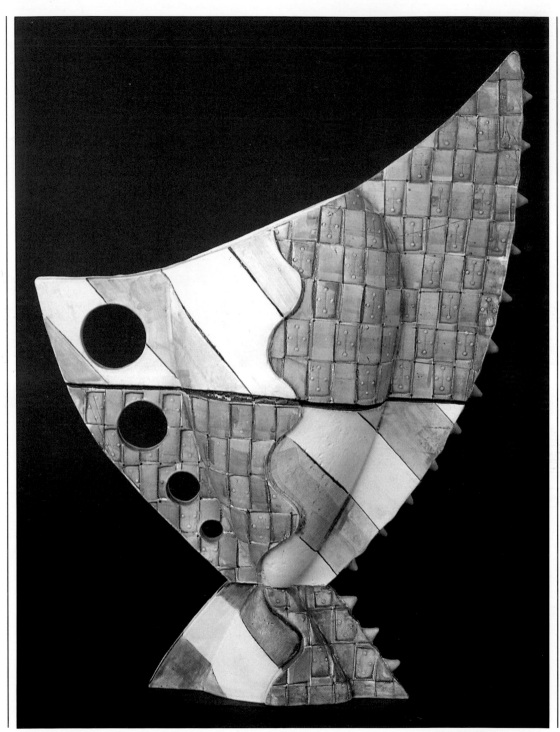

CAROL JACOBS
Handbuilt form
This sculptural earthenware
piece is an exploration of the
vessel form. Commercially
prepared colored stains were
used for the rich surface pattern,
and a form of drape mold
produced the shape.

ELSA RADY
Conjugations
Still life groups
The technical skill required to
throw these porcelain-shaped
vessels is considerable, but is
only part of the importance of
these works. Rady has grouped
together pieces of her work so
that they form spatial unit
relationships.

PAUL SOLDNER
Sculptural piece
This low-fired, unglazed piece
was partly thrown before
undergoing quite radical
alterations including cutting and
total reassembly (see ALTERING
THROWN SHAPES). Slips and
coloring stains were used on the
clay surface, and salt was
introduced to the firing.

◀ VIROT
Object
This French potter uses the sculptural potential of coarse open-bodied clay and slab building as the major elements. The use of a dark neutral gray stoneware glaze adds to the monumental qualities of this sculptural piece.

▶ LUGETTI
Abstract piece
In this simple yet powerful abstract composition, the contrasts of light against dark, plain surfaces against textured ones, and torn edges juxtaposed with precise ones provide constant visual interest.

► GYOZO LORINCZ
Picture

This potter treats his oxidized
stoneware panel in much the
same way as a modern abstract
painter might use paint on a
canvas.

► NORA BLAZEVICIUTE
Birds and stones

This potter has partly abstracted
her bird forms so that they
maintain their essential
characteristics in a simplified yet
recognizable manner. The
stoneware pieces, reduction fired
and glazed, are most effective
when seen as grouped units.

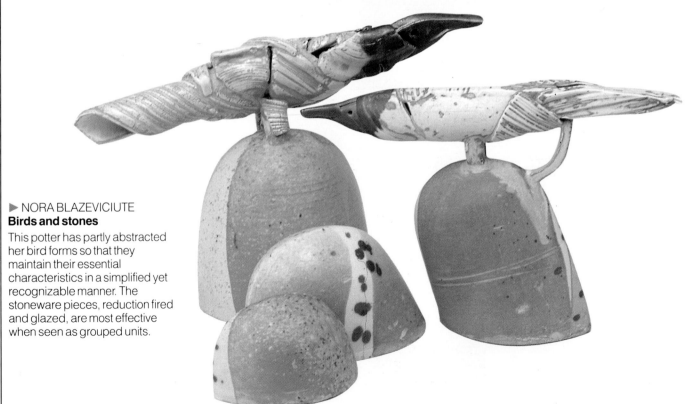

MAMEDOV ELDAR MURSAL
OGLY
**Object (painted glazed
stoneware)**

This potter uses color, shapes,
and symbols in his sculptural
forms which contain powerful
clues to his cultural background.

OPEN FORMS

One of the simplest forms, and one which lends itself well to a great variety of decorative treatments, is an open form, a generic term encompassing virtually any plate- or bowl-shaped piece. Such forms are produced for an almost infinite number of uses and reasons. They include the functional and domestic utilitarian objects from which we all eat to pieces which are partially or even completely divorced from function.

When pottery is produced by one of the semi-industrial processes such as SLIP CASTING, PRESS MOLDING, JIGGER AND JOLLY, and even EXTRUSION to a lesser extent, the shape and dimensions of a form are achieved as part of the process, but hand-forming techniques and THROWING by their very nature encourage the production of open forms. Handbuilt pots are often made by squeezing and pressing clay, which thins it, thus making the shape expand and grow outward. In the technique of PINCHING, for example, the clay wall is gently squeezed as the shape is rotated steadily in the hand. Coiled shapes will also grow rapidly outward if the coils are squeezed as part of the joining process (see COILING); indeed, this is one of the common problems of beginners, who want their pots to grow upward but find them growing outward instead.

When throwing on the wheel, the centrifugal force exerted on the clay as it rotates naturally pushes the shape open, and the potter who wants a narrow or tall shape has to work consciously against the natural inclinations of the clay. If clay were to be left to its own devices, a form which had begun to open would continue to do so until it became too wide to support itself, at which point it would collapse.

Thus open form is to a large extent the consequence of allowing or encouraging clay to do what comes most naturally to its particular qualities. It is knowledge of the material and skilful use of its potentialities that enable potters to produce such a diverse range and variety of shapes derived from a deceptively simple basic form.

For some potters, the intrinsic qualities of pure shape and form provide sufficient reason to explore personal definitions of open forms. Such considerations as the proportional relationships between the elements of a bowl or dish become all-important, obscuring others such as surface decoration. The deep handbuilt bowls of John Ward, for example, are first and foremost an investigation of shape for its own sake, a careful definition and refinement of the bowl as form, volume, and contained space. The bowl forms of potters such as Alan Caiger-Smith and Sutton Taylor, on the other hand, although no less skilfully made, are seen more as vehicles on which to exercise an individual style of surface decoration. The results in such cases can be quite spectacular, as the decoration itself develops as a means of further exploration of form. Alan Caiger-Smith's skilful use of lustered brushstrokes over a white earthenware glaze is a good illustration of the high standard of design it is possible to achieve. His flowing, direct, and assured handling of the brush has developed over many years into a powerful calligraphic sense of design.

In sharp contrast are potters whose forms offer neither utilitarian nor decorative surface potential, such as Ian Byers and Johan Van Loon. Their sculptural work is more concerned with a personal exploration and expression of the open form as it relates to the notion of space and volume.

Dorothy Feibleman explores the open form as a vehicle for her highly individual technique, derived from marquetry. This combines decoration with actual structure, so that the means she uses to create her bowl forms also gives them their highly patterned qualities.

◄ ALAN CAIGER-SMITH
Hand-thrown bowl, white tin glaze over red earthenware
The calligraphic luster brushwork on this bowl is used economically to explore the internal volume of the form. The design is a simple one, which relies to a large extent on the balance between the width and strength of lines in relation to the white background areas of the glazed surface. Although appearing simple, such a design can only be really successful if the brushmarks are fluid and surely applied, as here.

► GERRY UNSWORTH
Porcelain bowl with pink luster
This small bowl shows a careful balance in proportion and shape. The bowl springs strongly from the turned foot, defining a satisfying volume as it grows, and is brought to a fitting conclusion by the slightly flaring rim which reflects the outward-flowing tendency of wheel-formed shapes.

PETER LANE
Porcelain bowl with wave decoration

Lane has skilfully employed carved and incised undulating layered bands on the outer surface of his thrown porcelain bowl. The pattern, suggesting the movement of waves, is further emphasized by the subtle carving of the rim and the considered use of a pale blue celadon glaze, which allows the carving to remain clearly visible. The piece was reduction fired at 2336°F (1280°C).

PETER LANE
Porcelain bowl with tree design

The pierced and carved band of tree decoration (see PIERCED DECORATION) makes a strong visual impact in this piece. The simplified shapes were derived from observation of intertwining branches and trunks in hedges, demonstrating how ideas for interesting work can be found almost anywhere. Care has been taken in considering where to pierce through the design without causing undue weakening of the structure. The bowl was fired in an electric kiln to 2300°F (1260°C).

SUTTON TAYLOR
Lustered earthenware bowl

The surface patterns here have been derived from a variety of sources, one being the effect of light through overlapping translucent leaves. The surface decoration conveys a natural, curved but spiky quality evocative of wild plants growing in unhindered profusion.

The base glaze was fired to a temperature of 2048°F (1120°C), and after the application of lustered decoration, the bowl was again fired in a reduction atmosphere to a temperature of about 1382°F (750°C). This caused the original glaze to melt just sufficiently for the luster to fuse into it.

SUTTON TAYLOR
Lustered bowl (detail)

This shows the rich combination of color and surface texture that Taylor achieves in his work.

JOHN ABLITT
Burnished bowl

This piece is crisp, clean edged, and very modern in its design. The highly decorative inner area, containing elements of textile design, provides both contrast and visual relief from the severity of the black areas that surround it. The bowl was press molded and decorated with a number of colored slips. When leather-hard, it was burnished and then fired to a temperature of 1832°F (1000°C).

DAVID JONES
Thrown raku bowl

The necessarily coarse, open nature of the RAKU body used for this bowl is clearly visible in the stark black bands that run across the surface. This blackening occurs when unglazed areas are reduced in sawdust or similar material immediately after the raku FIRING. They form a powerful element of the design here, and are emphasized by the cut rim. This draws the eye naturally to the point at which the lines begin, and thence across the whole surface.

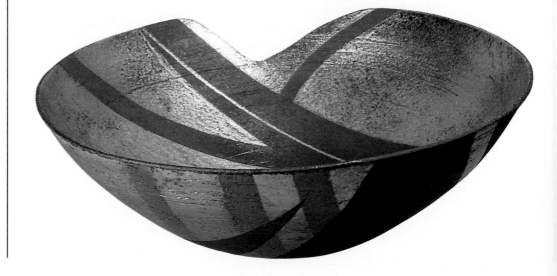

IAN BYERS
Beaked form

The process of COILING used to produce this form allows the shape to develop in a very natural way, and the potter has accentuated this effect by his use of slips in conjunction with burnished, lustered, and smoked surfaces (see BURNISHING and SMOKING). The form has a quiet, contemplative quality about it which encourages the viewer to consider the shape in relation to its exploration of volume and space. The bowl is part of a series of work on the same theme.

▲ ELSA RADY
Porcelain bowl form

This potter has used a glaze which has produced an interesting, heavily textured surface, in surprising contrast to the precise, edged quality of the form. Some of Rady's pieces, with their careful shaping and "winged" appearance, suggest the idea of flight.

◄ ELSA RADY
Fingerprints

Both the shapes and the uncompromising colors used by this potter convey a feeling of the tensions and mechanical forces of modern life. Her thinly thrown porcelain forms, something of a technical feat in themselves, are frequently cut and shaped (see FLUTING) in a way that imitates the qualities of sharp-edged metal.

ELSA RADY
Bowl
Much of Rady's work is characterized by flat, often brash colors applied so evenly that they look almost like sprayed paint on the surface of sheet metal.

◀▶ DOROTHY FEIBLEMAN
Bowls
The forming and decorative techniques used to produce these bowls are in this case one and the same. They are made from carefully arranged segments of different colored clays, laminated together and formed painstakingly within a mold lined with a sheet of thin clay. When the shape is complete, the inside and protective outer layer of clay are carefully scraped to reveal the crisp design on both inner and outer surfaces. The bowl on the left suggests organic qualities such as those of rocks, plants, and vegetables, while the geometric patterning of those on the right demonstrates precision that can be obtained by PRESS MOLDING techniques. The high failure rate of Feibleman's method is increased by her use of spaces within the structures, which makes them even more vulnerable to breakage.

LUCIE RIE
Thrown bowl
The delicate pink blush and thin incised lines radiating from the center, encased between the bands of heavy color at rim and foot, are reminiscent of fungi, as is the honest simplicity of the form.

JOHN WARD
Deep handbuilt bowl

Ward is a potter whose preoccupation with a continuing exploration of the basic bowl shape has led him to put considerations of form above those of function. The piece is decorated with radiating bands of green emerging through a matt white glaze.

MARY RICH
Thrown bowl

The angular nature of this highly decorative piece is echoed in the striking geometric gold lustered patterns which embellish both inner and outer surfaces.

ENCLOSED AND NARROWED FORMS

To produce enclosed forms the potter has to resolve a variety of technical problems specific to this kind of shape. The method of production must also be carefully considered, since factors relating to handbuilt enclosed forms are not the same as those which affect similar forms produced by throwing or casting from molds.

Hand-forming techniques such as COILING are a popular method of construction for the type of form which narrows or totally closes over, but the problem arises of how to support the weight of overhanging sections. As mentioned in the first section of the book, each new coil needs to be placed slightly inside the preceding one, thus allowing the shape to narrow and close. The clay must be soft enough to permit easy joining of the sections, but if it is too soft, an inward-turning shape may very easily collapse. This problem can be resolved in a number of ways. Loosely-packed newspaper can be used to support the clay as the shape is built up, or alternately, the base section can be left to stiffen while the section which is being built is kept damp and workable. A hairdryer can be used to speed up the stiffening process; some potters even use blow torches. In less sophisticated cultures, potters use a variation of the same method, placing hot coals or embers into the bottom of the pot so that it hardens while the top part remains workable. David Roberts, who is well known for his production of large RAKU-fired bottles, overcomes the problem by working on several bottles at the same time. This not only allows them to stiffen as they are worked on, but has the additional advantage of enabling the potter to produce a number of closely related shapes which form an identifiable group.

Enclosed or narrowed forms pose particular problems if they are produced by SLIP CASTING or PRESS MOLDING. The nature of the shape means that overhangs would be created in the mold which would make it impossible to remove the pot, so these forms, whether spherical or bottle shapes, always require at least a two-piece mold or sometimes a more complex one.

In THROWING, the potter is faced with a direct test of skill. When an open or bowl-like form is thrown, the centrifugal force created by the rotating wheel works in the potter's favor, but with an enclosed or narrowed shape he or she must work against the natural inclination of the rotating clay. COLLARING plays an important part in the production of such shapes. The extra thickness in the clay wall which is a natural consequence of the process is either used up as the form continues to close and grow inward or, in the case of bottle shapes, can be used to increase the height of the neck. Potters who throw bottle or enclosed forms on the wheel often inflate the thrown shape immediately after throwing by blowing gently into it to increase its fullness. The neck can then be sealed if narrow enough, so that the air maintains the rounded shape until the clay has stiffened. It is common practice to leave the base section of enclosed or bottle forms relatively thick to act as a support for overhanging clay. The excess thickness can be removed by TURNING when the pot has reached the leather-hard stage.

Many potters who work on the wheel include the bottle or enclosed form in their regular repertoire. Derek Clarkson is one such potter, who is well known for his continuous development and refinement of the thrown bottle form.

Like all pottery forms, enclosed or narrowed shapes can be produced as a variety of functional items. Bottles and flasks, among the most common, are found as basic pottery forms throughout all cultures and periods of history, but purely decorative forms, or explorations of more abstract ideas, are equally valid in this context, and many items may fall into two or more of these categories at the same time. A spherical or partly enclosed shape, for example, can provide a basis for ideas about shape and particular decorative treatments, while still being partly or even totally functional.

DAVID LEACH
Rounded form

This form narrows to a
well-defined rim which acts like a
period. The dark-colored iron-
bearing glaze breaks through the
lighter one to create additional
surface interest.

◀ HARVEY SADOW
Sacred sites (Australia series)
Color and texture are both employed to excellent effect in this RAKU vessel. The rich combination of vibrant color and surface was achieved by multiple firings and sandblasting of the surface at various stages.

▶ HARVEY SADOW
Ground zero series
This potter's masterful use of combined slips, sandblasting, and multiple RAKU firings have given this piece a feeling of agelessness. The partly etched surface is the direct result of sandblasting, while the raku firing process has produced the rich bronzed and blackened surface.

DAVID ROBERTS
Bottle forms

These bottles by the RAKU potter
David Roberts were coiled
(see COILING) and worked on
simultaneously. The subtle
variations in proportion, shape,
and degree of surface crackle are
important to the cohesion of the
pieces into a group.

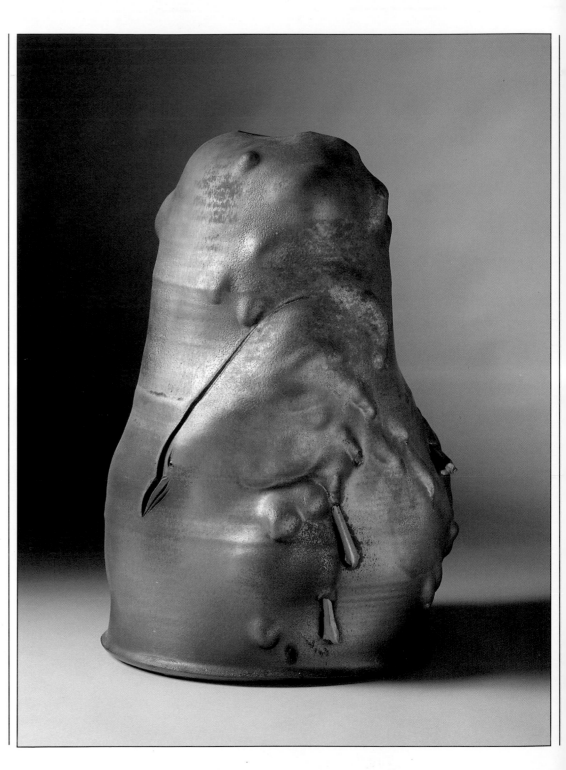

FRANK BOYDEN
Raven trap

This thrown narrowed form has provided the basis for an intriguing if slightly macabre surface treatment. The piece was made from stoneware clay incorporating porcelain "bird bones," which project from the surface. The rich bronze surface glaze was heavily saturated with manganese and copper, and the piece was wood fired (see FIRING).

FRANK BOYDEN
Dead salmon vase
This porcelain piece is unglazed;
the rich color variations are a
direct result of the wood FIRING,
with the paler coloring down
one side caused by a heavy
ash deposit.

▲ PETER BEARD
Pot

The rich surface texture and patterning was achieved by a combination of sponging on color and wax resist techniques (see RESIST DECORATION). White slip was coated on to provide a light base. After the bisque firing, a layer of glaze was added, and more was applied with a sponge to build up the surface. The pattern was defined by wax resist, with further glaze and colors on top.

◄ PETER COSENTINO
Large burnished bottle

This thrown form was covered with slip made from a locally dug clay prior to BURNISHING. The tiny neck was left uneven to emphasize the natural qualities of the shape. The surface was smoked (see SMOKING) in a sawdust kiln after bisque firing.

◄ HANS COPER
Tall bottle form
This piece shows a carefully considered balance between shape, form, and texture. The rich textural areas are emphasized with manganese, which creates a strong contrast to the off-white colored slip of the body.

▼ PETER COSENTINO
Small rounded pot
This piece was thrown, sliced, and altered, with sections inserted to maintain the shape and seal the two parts. It was then burnished and lightly smoked (see BURNISHING and SMOKING).

PICTORIAL AND NARRATIVE FORMS

Whatever the construction process chosen, a shallow plate or dish form is one of the more simple shapes to make. Because such shapes are only slightly raised, the problems of stability and balance are avoided. Their shallowness also makes them relatively easy to decorate in considerable detail, and surfaces can be exploited to good effect as vehicles for pictorial or narrative forms of decoration. Shallow forms are not, of course, the only possibility for this type of treatment, but they are particularly well suited to it.

The use of pottery surfaces as a vehicle for story-telling is nothing new, and some of the best examples have come from early Greek pottery and the decorative *maiolica* wares of Italy (see MAJOLICA).

Early Greek pottery was famed for its figurative decoration relating contemporary events and customs such as weddings, funerals, and sporting activities as well as mythological narratives. Complete stories are told in great visual detail: Herakles killing the centaur, Perseus beheading the gorgon Medusa, Achilles caught in the act of killing Troilus, and many tales of the gods and goddesses.

Maiolica, a highly "painterly" decorated tin-glazed ware, became extremely popular in Italy during the 15th and 16th centuries, and spread to many other parts of Europe. Narrative scenes were depicted with astonishing skill, with the pottery painters treating their surfaces as a painter will treat a canvas. There were various different styles of decoration, among them *istoriato* (story painting) and one known as "decorative style" or "beautiful style," and subjects included stories based on popular mythological and religious themes and scenes from everyday life.

For modern potters the choices are equally wide. Some may illustrate stories or make social comment through their work as well as using their surfaces as a means of using decorative skills. Many potters tell stories through pictures in a directly narrative manner, though normally employing a less intricate style than that seen on Italian *maiolica*. The old adage "every picture tells a story" applies as much to pottery as to

JOSIE WALTER
Oval dish with chicken decoration

The part stylized, part cartoon characteristics of this wry bird are expertly rendered through the use of paper resist and slip (see RESIST DECORATION and SLIP DECORATION).

any other visual art form, although in some cases it might be more accurate to say that "every picture tells part of a story," as some decorations will hint at a narrative rather than telling it in full. There is perhaps a greater tendency today to refrain from unfolding a whole tale. A simplified image, a semi-abstract symbol, or some clue in the title of the piece are often the only clues given to the meaning of an illustrative surface or narrative element; the rest is left to the imagination of the viewer. An example is the work of Dennis Parks, who employs symbolic imagery such as strongly graphic hands on the surfaces of his large plates. His titles, "How they Brought the Good News from Ghent to Aix," or "Random Pleasures" convey

JOSIE WALTER
Packet of fish
This potter's work is in red earthenware clay, and incorporates both traditional and contemporary methods of SLIP DECORATION, including paper resist (see RESIST DECORATION) with slip infill, trailing, and brush decoration. Her work is raw glazed and fired to approximately 2012°F (1100°C) in an electric kiln. This piece contains a gentle underlying humor which is carried through the expressions on the faces of the "happy" fish.

enough specific information to tell the viewer that a narrative of some kind is present.

A variety of techniques can be used for this form of decoration. The potential of the *maiolica* method has already been mentioned, and the work of Andrew McGarva is a good example of this. It is interesting to note, however, that this potter employs a different firing method to that used for *maiolica*, although his work is in many respects in keeping with the *maiolica* and delftware traditions, particularly the latter, in his characteristic use of a restricted, predominantly blue palette. He works at stoneware temperatures, whereas traditional *maiolica* and delftware were fired at earthenware temperatures only.

The variety and range of techniques associated with SLIP DECORATION also offer great potential for illustrative surfaces. Common pictorial subjects for 17th-century slipware dishes included popular themes such as "The Pelican in her Piety," "Mermaid Combing her Hair," and "Adam and Eve," and there were also portraits of eminent contemporary figures. The work of modern potters such as John Pollex and Josie Walter shows the influence of traditional styles, although their work is more sophisticated.

Another popular method for specific themes or visual effects is the use of modeled or relief work. Potter Frank Boyden makes use of this technique to interpret his powerful semi-abstract ideas.

◄ ANDREW McGARVA
Hen bowl
The body is stoneware, and hen and surrounding decoration were painted onto the glaze surface using a combination of cobalt oxide (for the blue), iron oxide (for the brown), and titanium dioxide (for the yellow). The decorative technique has many similarities with those associated with English delftware.

► FRANK BOYDEN
Salmon birth
This large plate was fired to stoneware temperature in a wood-fired kiln in which the entire plate was covered in charcoal during the firing. This caused the color variations. The salmon head was cast in porcelain, and there is an evident symbolism in the way it emerges, breaking through the surface of the clay.

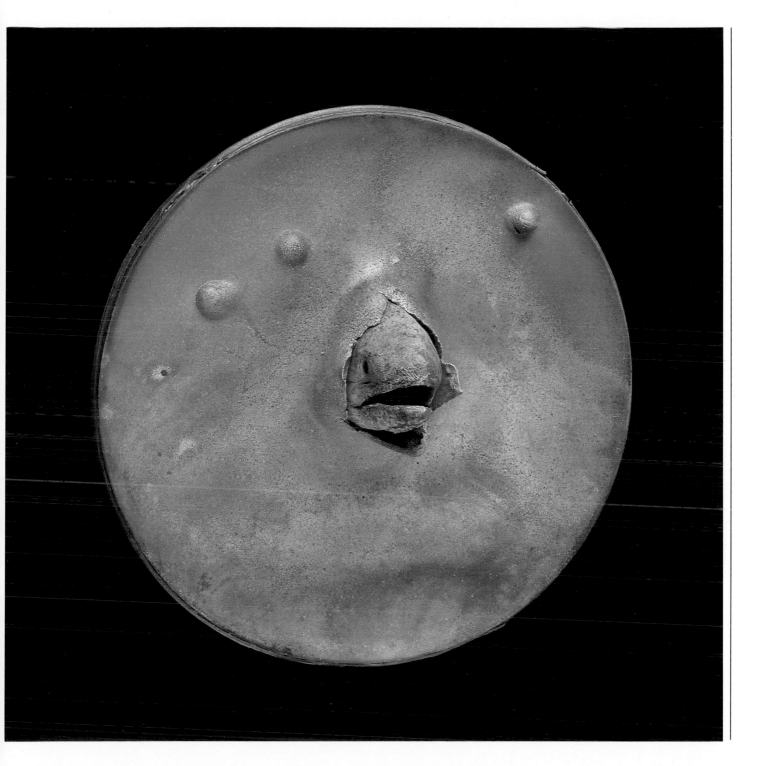

▲ DENNIS PARKS
How they brought the good news from Ghent to Aix

Large plates offer potters a surface which cries out for decoration just as a canvas does for painting. Parks uses a combination of metal oxides and neutral-colored glazes to produce very individual surface pictures with a hint of narrative content. This piece was fired to stoneware temperature in an oil-fired kiln (see FIRING).

▶ DENNIS PARKS
Random Pleasures

This large thrown plate, like many other similar pieces by this potter, makes use of the emotive associations of the hands, which combine with the titles to provide clues about stories lying behind them. There is always sufficient ambiguity, however, for the viewer to interpret them in his or her own way.

CHRISTA-MARIA HERRMANN
Globe

This piece displays a masterly
use of the RAKU technique to
convey a sense of multilateralism.
To produce an enclosed form
such as this, raku cooling must
take place gradually to ensure
the piece does not split open;
instead of being immersed in
water, the piece is thrust into
damp sawdust.

THE FIGURE

Of the infinite potential sources of inspiration available to us, the human figure is perhaps the one most frequently drawn on. Artists, sculptors, and potters have all been fascinated by the human figure, and some have devoted most of their working lives to depicting it. Representations of the figure in clay can be traced back thousands of years, to objects which are known to have been produced considerably earlier than the first pottery vessels. Prehistoric clay figures were associated with religious and magical ritual, many being produced as fertility symbols, to ensure good crops or productive child-bearing. These, still produced in some less developed cultures today, were modeled from clay and baked in a fire to harden them. Many clay figures and painted decorations on pottery have provided evidence for social customs and practices, giving the historian valuable insights into aspects of past cultures. For example, depictions of people carrying out everyday activities are commonly found in ancient Egyptian and Eastern ceramics, while the painted wares of the Greek and Roman worlds depict with great accuracy the events, customs, and styles of dress particular to the time. Such themes are, of course, still as pertinent today as they were in the past.

The modern age has seen the emergence of great debates over the definition of pottery and ceramic work, and whether some pieces should be described as sculpture, ceramics, or pottery. However, the point at which something fashioned in clay ceases to be pottery and becomes sculpture is not easy to assess, and often the only sense to be made of the issue is by a subjective assessment of personal feelings toward the work, regardless of any artificial category. However, contemporary exponents whose work falls into the somewhat gray area often described as "figurative sculpture," tend to sit uneasily among other potters. Some of their work sets out to explore such different ideas to those of more traditional potters that any comparison is meaningless.

The work of potters such as Jill Crowley and Glenys Barton is well known for its exploration into and involvement with the human figure. Crowley's work features a slightly humorous observation of "city gentlemen," – isolated figures, coil modeled (see COILING) from coarse RAKU clays whose impurities bleed through to the surface and create pitted textural skins. By comparison, the figures of Glenys Barton convey a contemplative quality. They are often removed from any obvious sexual context, sometimes devoid of hair, or of facial or other gender-determining physical features. She often uses the raku technique in order to add aging qualities to her work.

As with any subject, the way the figure is depicted varies enormously, determined by the ideas and preoccupations of the maker. Some figures are completely realistic, with every detail shown with strict accuracy, while others may be treated in a semi-abstract way. Similarly, one potter may decide on a three-dimensional treatment, while another prefers to restrict the figurative elements to surface decoration.

Where the figure is used in the latter way, as in the work of Sandy Brown, the processes used are the same as for any other form of decoration (see DECORATING). Nor is there any special construction method for this kind of work; most of the forming techniques can be adapted to figurative work, although both the THROWING and JIGGER AND JOLLY processes are obviously of limited use in this context. Jill Crowley is one of many potters who use COILING as a means of producing a hollow basic shape onto which features are modeled. SLABBING and even processes such as SLIP CASTING (a technique often used by Glenys Barton) or EXTRUSION of shapes from which to build also have their applications. All these processes involve the production of a hollow piece of work, thus eliminating the technical problems associated with firing solid or very thick clay sections.

It is, of course, possible to build up the basic shape as a solid and add further pellets of clay, in which case there are several simple methods of ensuring that the work can be fired safely. A coarse, open-bodied clay

SANDY BROWN
Jolly lady
This highly colorful stoneware
dish uses the figure as a two-
dimensional decorative device.
The loose approach to the
painting, in which anatomical
accuracy has little relevance, is a
reflection of the potter's interest in
the expression of personal
emotions and feelings.

should be used, as this will permit thicker sections to
be fired in the normal way. Where a section is more
than about 1½in (3.8cm) thick, excess clay should be
removed while still soft enough to permit this, but dry
enough to avoid any danger of collapse. An
alternative is to use the same kind of clay to produce a
solid object, which is allowed to dry out thoroughly
over a long period of time and then fired extremely
slowly. It is perfectly possible to fire solid shapes;

bricks, for example, are fired as a matter of course.
However, in a brick firing the drying and firing
process is extended over a continuous period of
weeks, a much longer time than normal for other
types of pottery firing.

MARIA KUCZYNSKA
Porcelain bust
This piece was constructed from layers and slabs of porcelain. The Polish potter Kuczynska makes effective use of light and dark: the features on half of the face are suggested through shadows thrown by carefully planned raised areas, which create the illusion of features.

CARMEN DIONYSE
Dust

This powerful piece by the Belgian potter/sculptor has a strong sense of timelessness, but there is also a disturbing ambiguity. Is it an obvious reference to death and mummification, or could it be a symbol of rebirth, with the new form about to emerge from the old?

EVA KUN
Women
Personal comment on political
and social issues has always
been a part of some artists' and
potters' work. Here the Pierrot-like
bandaged image creates a
strong feeling of sad loneliness.

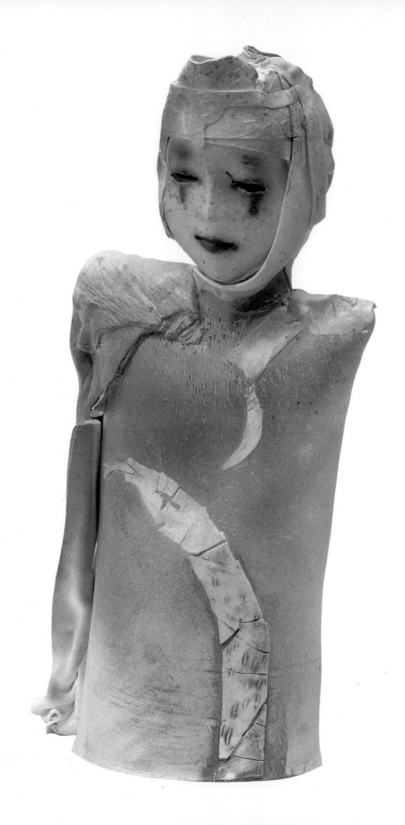

IMRE SCHRAMMEL
Minotaur
This prominent Hungarian potter's piece is highly detailed, and although only about 15¾in (40cm) in height, has a monumental feeling. The heavy coating of oxides provides a surface coloring which enhances the sculptural qualities. Heavily grogged stoneware clay (see ADDITIVES) was used, fired in a reduction atmosphere to 2336°F (1280°C).

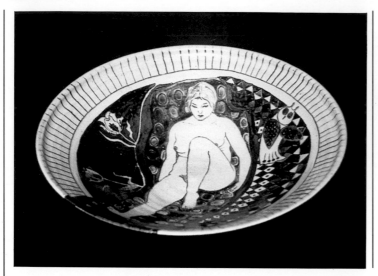

◄ ERIC MELLON
Bowl in stoneware
This potter's work employs figurative designs developed from his love of figure drawings drawn directly from the nude. The designs are painted in oxides onto fresh ash-glazed surfaces. In this piece the rich patterned qualities of the decoration combine satisfyingly with the main central figure of the female nude.

▼ ERIC MELLON
Theme of tenderness
A mermaid with fish tail and human legs, entwined lovers, moon goddesses, and foxes are all recurring ideas in Eric Mellon's work. These themes form the surface decoration on this bowl.

JILL CROWLEY
Man in blue shirt (detail)
The coarse open-bodied clays
used by Jill Crowley contain a
high proportion of iron which
oozes through the clay surface
during firing, and is clearly
evident in this head. For many of
her clay busts she uses a type
of coiling technique to produce a
hollow form, onto which facial and
other detail is then modeled. She
uses slips and color to add
further definition to both flesh and
clothing detail.

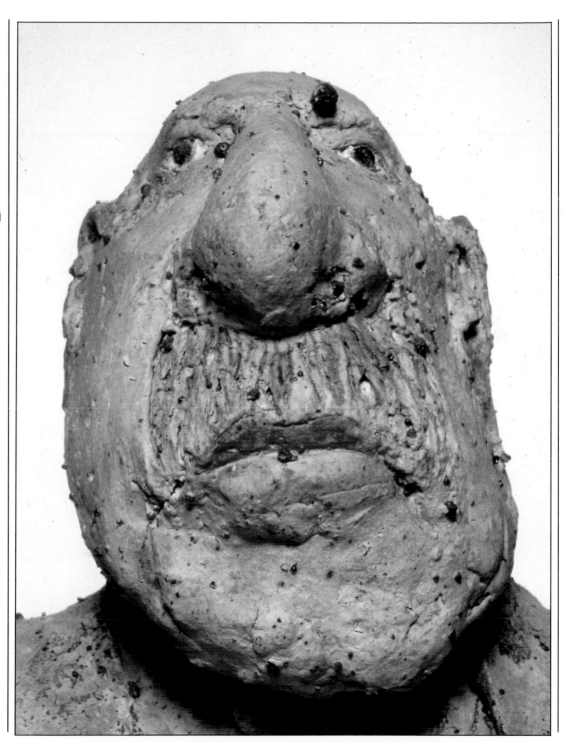

LASZLO FEKETE
Plastic

The figure here has been
reduced to the main elements of
head, hand, and foot, setting up a
continuous contrast between the
rounded flesh qualities and the
angular rock-like structure of the
torso. The piece is colored
stoneware, which was fired to
2336°F (1280°C) in an electric kiln.

AGNES BOZSOGI
Small raku figure
The two distinctively different qualities of informal and formal are combined in this work, with the heavy, loosely modeled torso balancing precariously on the rigid geometric structure below.

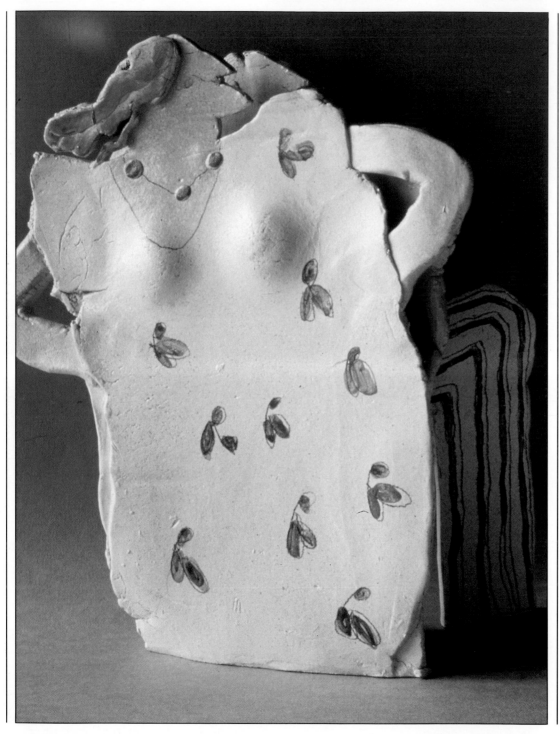

RUTH FRANKLIN
Dancers
Ruth Franklin conveys gentle humor in her portrayal of the human figure. In this piece made largely from slabs, the stance and body position transmit a wonderful arrogance which this potter/sculptor has captured with the minimum of fuss or detail. Color, which is used sparingly, is applied in the form of an underglaze.

SANDOR KECSKEMETI
Head

This potter has reduced the idea of the head down to its fundamental abstract elements. The influences of artists such as Arp, Miró, Picasso, and Henry Moore can all be seen in this piece.

RUTH FRANKLIN
Man drinking a pint of Guinness

This slab built, earthenware fired figure was inspired by a series of drawings made over a period of time. The man who is in clay sits on a wooden base and upright; the table is in perspex. The figure is painted but a chocolate wrapper has been used to define his arm.

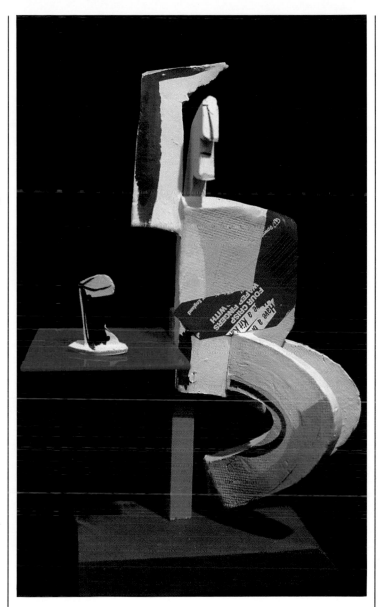

CREDITS

Every effort has been made to obtain copyright clearance, and we do apologise if any omissions have been made. The author and Quarto would like to thank the following artists for their co-operation.

Title verso Frank Boyden; **p7** Peter Cosentino; **p12** Peter Cosentino; **p13** Judith Wooton; **p14** Galerie Besson/Lucie Rie; **p15** *(top)* Galerie Besson/Hans Coper; *(bottom)* Peter Cosentino; **p16** Kenneth Bright; **p17** Mary Rich; **p20** Magdalene Odundo; **p22** Peter Cosentino; **p24** *(top)* Fiona Salazar; *(bottom)* David Roberts; **p25** John Leach; **p26** *(top)* Sandy Brown; *(bottom)* Galerie Besson/Lucie Rie; **p27** *(top)* Michael Bayley; *(bottom left)* John Glick; *(bottom right)* Frank Boyden; **p28** Peter Cosentino; **p29** *(top)* Dart Pottery/Janice Tchalenko; *(bottom)* John Glick; **p30** *(left)* Galerie Besson/Elizabeth Frisch; *(bottom)* Crafts Council/Dennis Parks; **p31** *(top left)* John Gibson; *(top right)* Daphne Carnegy; *(bottom)* Jo Connell; **p32** *(top)* Mary Wondrausch; *(bottom)* Karen Chesney; **p33** *(top)* Daphne Carnegy; *(middle)* Sandy Brown; *(bottom)* Christa-Maria Herrmann; **p34** Andrew McGarva; **p35** Victoria and Albert Museum, London; **p36** John Glick; **p37** Janet Leach; **p40** Jo Burton; **p41** *(left)* Barbara Cass; *(top)* Swiss National Museum, Zurich/Elsie Blumer; **p44** Walter Keeler; **p45** Gus Mabelson; **p46** Carol Jacobs; **p47** Peter Lane; **p48** Harrison McIntosh; **p49** Jo Connell; **p50** Sabena Teuteberg; **p51** Sabena Teuteberg; **p55** Gerry Unsworth; **p56** Seth Cardew; **p58** Daphne Carnegy; **p60** Peter Lane; **p62** John Ablitt; **p63** Jo Connell; **p66** Peter Cosentino; **p67** *(top)* Frank Boyden; *(left)* David Roberts; *(right)* Harvey Sadow; **p68** *(top)* Josie Walter; *(bottom)* Peter Beard; **p69** Peter Cosentino; **p71** Jenny Clarke; **p73** *(top)* Michael Bayley; *(bottom)* Steven Hill; **p75** Steven Hill; **p76** *(bottom right)* John Gibson; **p77** *(top right)* Peter Cosentino; **p78** Peter Cosentino; **p79** *(bottom)* Magdalene Odundo; *(middle right)* Steven Hill; **p80** Wedgwood; **p83** *(top)* Galerie Besson/Lucie Rie; *(middle)* Peter Cosentino; *(bottom)* Galerie Besson/Hans Coper; **p85** *(bottom left)* Seth Cardew; **p87** Gerry Unsworth; **p89** *(middle left)* Peter Lane; *(top right)* Sutton Taylor; **p97** Elsa Rady; **p98** *(top right)* Crafts Council/Mary Rogers; *(top left and bottom)* Michael Bayley; **p99** Jo Connell; **p100** *(left and bottom)* Magdalene Odundo; **p101** Magdalene Odundo; **p102** Barbara Manuel; **p103** *(left)* Karen Chesney; *(right)* Peter Lane; **p104** *(left)* David Jones; *(top)* Swiss National Museum, Zurich/G. Weigel; **p105** Swiss National Museum, Zurich/Ives Motty; **p106** *(top and left)* Christine Constant; **p107** Christine Constant; **p108** Mike Golding/Christine Constant; **p109** Mike Golding/Christine Constant; **p111** Crafts Council/Svend Bayer; **p112** *(top and right)* Jenny Clarke; **p113** Jenny Clarke; **p114** *(top)* Crafts Council/Jane Hamlyn; *(bottom)* Gus Mabelson; **p115** Gerry Unsworth; **p116** *(left and right)* Daphne Carnegy; **p117** Dart Pottery; **p118** *(top and bottom)* Sabina Teuteberg; **p119** Sabina Teuteberg; **p120** Steven Hill; **p121** Steven Hill; **p122** Walter Keeler; **p123** *(top and right)* Walter Keeler; **p124** *(left)* David Scott; *(right)* Sabina Teuteberg; **p125** Sabina Teuteberg; **p127** Harvey Sadow; **p128** *(top and bottom)* Marian Gaunce; **p129** Karen Norquay/Marian Gaunce; **p130** *(left)* Peter Lane; *(bottom)* John Leach; **p131** John Leach; **p132** Felicity Aylieff; **p133** *(top)* Archie McCall; *(bottom)* Felicity Aylieff; **p134** *(top)* Swiss National Museum, Zurich/Elsie Blumer; **p134** *(bottom)* Swiss National Museum, Zurich/Kristiansen; **p135** Swiss National Museum, Zurich/Elsie Blumer; **p136** Sabina Teuteberg; **p137** Sabina Teuteberg; **p138** *(top)* Janet Leach; *(bottom)* Galerie Besson/Elizabeth Fritsch; **p139** Galerie Besson/Elizabeth Fritsch; **p141** *(top)* Crafts Council/Colin Pearson; *(left)* Peter Cosentino; **p142** Frank Boyden; **p143** Galerie Besson/Hans Coper; **p144** Carol Jacobs; **p145** Elsa Rady; **p146** Paul Soldner; **p147** *(top)* Swiss National Museum, Zurich/Virot; *(bottom)* Swiss National Museum, Zurich/Lugetti; **p148** *(top)* International Ceramic Studio, Hungary/Gyozo Lorincz; *(bottom)* International Ceramic Studio, Hungary/Nora Blazeviciute; **p149** International Ceramic Studio, Hungary/Mamedov Eldar Mursal Ogly; **p151** *(top)* Crafts Council/Alan Caiger-Smith; *(bottom)* Gerry Unsworth; **p152** *(top and bottom)* Peter Lane; **p153** *(top and bottom)* Sutton Taylor; **p154** *(top)* John Ablitt; *(bottom)* David Jones; **p155** Ian Byers; **p156** *(top and bottom)* Elsa Rady; **p157** Elsa Rady; **p158** Dorothy Feibleman; **p159** Dorothy Feibleman; **p160** Galerie Besson/Lucie Rie; **p161** *(top)* John Ward; *(bottom)* Mary Rich; **p163** David Leach; **p164** *(top and bottom)* Harvey Sadow; **p165** David Roberts; **p166** Frank Boyden; **p167** Frank Boyden; **p168** *(top)* Peter Beard; *(bottom)* Peter Cosentino; **p169** *(left)* Galerie Besson/Hans Coper; *(bottom)* Peter Cosentino; **p170** Josie Walter; **p171** Josie Walter; **p172** Andrew McGarva; **p173** Frank Boyden; **p174** Dennis Parks; **p175** Christa-Maria Herrmann; **p177** Sandy Brown; **p178** Swiss National Museum, Zurich/Maria Kuczynska; **p179** Swiss National Museum, Zurich/Carmen Dionyse; **p180** International Ceramic Studio, Hungary/Eva Kun; **p181** International Ceramic Studio, Hungary/Imre Schrammel; **p182** *(top and bottom)* Crafts Council/Eric Mellon; **p183** Crafts Council/Jill Crowley; **p184** International Ceramic Studio, Hungary/Laszlo Fekete; **p185** International Ceramic Studio, Hungary/Agnes Bozsogi; **p186** Crafts Council/Ruth Franklin; **p187** *(left)* International Ceramic Studio, Hungary/Sandor Kecskemeti; *(right)* Ruth Franklin.

Chart **pp38-39** David Kemp.